# THE COMPLETE HOMESTEADING BOOK

THE COMPLETE
# HOMESTEADING
# BOOK *Proven Methods*
## *for Self-sufficient Living*

## by DAVID E. ROBINSON

ILLUSTRATED BY
PAULA SAVASTANO

Diagrams by Douglas Merrilees

**GARDEN WAY PUBLISHING**
*Charlotte, Vermont 05445*

*Library of Congress Catalog Card Number: 74-75462*
*ISBN 0-88266-029-2 paperback*
*ISBN 0-88266-030-6 casebound*

COPYRIGHT 1974 BY GARDEN WAY PUBLISHING CO.
CHARLOTTE, VERMONT 05445

*Sixth Printing, December 1977*

*Printed in the United States by Capital City Press*
*Montpelier, Vermont.*

# CONTENTS

# THE COMPLETE HOMESTEADING BOOK

CHAPTER ONE

# WHAT IS HOMESTEADING?

> *Such is the superiority of rural occupations and pleasures, that com-*
> *merce, large societies, or crowded cities, may be justly reckoned un-*
> *natural. Indeed, the very purpose for which we engage in commerce is,*
> *that we may be one day enabled to retire to the country, where alone*
> *we picture to ourselves days of solid satisfaction and undisturbed hap-*
> *piness. It is evident that such sentiments are natural to the human mind.*
> JOHN LOUDON, *A Treatise on*
> *Forming, Improving, and Managing*
> *Country Residences*, 1806.

In our imaginations, as well as in literature, we often carry an image of life in the country that is a conglomeration of our favorite fantasies. We see a "little place in the country" as the best reward for a life of city labor in "commerce," and as the realization of our deeply-felt hopes for what a pleasant life should be. Somehow (and perhaps such sentiments *are* "natural to the human mind") we regard country life as more complete than city life, its pleasures more natural and its rhythms more in tune with the seasons and with the earth. Country vs. city has been a standard literary conflict for hundreds of years; and almost always it is country life that wins the tussle.

9

What, then, is our image of country life? For people who feel trapped in a city the image is positively romantic: a little white farmhouse, a sturdy red barn, a few old maple trees, a colorful garden and perhaps a child's swing on an old apple tree out back. It may include a few chickens clucking contentedly at the back door, and of course a friendly old dog asleep in the shade. And there are sounds: the hum of bees, wind in the treetops, the clank of a cowbell from a distant pasture.

This image is appealing to be sure. Cities have always been relatively dirty and crowded; the smog of modern times has only replaced the street mire of a century ago. Today we have managed to crowd *more* people into the large cities, though the conditions of poverty may be slightly better. Certainly we have produced enough noise, smoke and traffic jams to make every city dweller turn longing eyes to the country for "peace and quiet," a slower pace and the feeling of soft road dust between his emancipated toes.

Today as we look at our cities we really do find an appalling situation. In older, more established places like Philadelphia we find an inner city area where murder is commonplace and where huge blocks of buildings stand abandoned and condemned. In more "futuristic" cities such as Los Angeles the inhabitants have escaped the concentration of a central area, but the result is that they move about enclosed in small glass and steel cubicles, isolated from a polluted sky, from the earth and from each other. The great freeways, built to promote speedy transport, developed traffic jams that often return the traveler to something slower than the speed of grandpa's horse and buggy.

The effect of this urban deterioration is to disenchant us with city life, and to bolster our image of the country as an escape—as an ideal, "natural" way of life. Removed as most of us are from the realities of rural living, we cling to a fantasy version of "life on the land," even embellishing the benefits of the country to the level of poetry. The dirt and dangers of city life take a poor second place to the imagined pleasures of the white farmhouse on a country lane.

THE BACK-TO-THE-LAND MOVEMENT

Partly because this country image is contrasted with city experience, a strong back-to-the-land movement undeniably is occurring. In a sense it started with the growth of the suburbs, which developed as attempts to enjoy a more rural existence within reach of city jobs. The movement back to the country largely is a movement of the children of suburbia, many of whom are refugees from academic careers and establishment living. They see the effort to combine city jobs and suburban joys as essentially futile—as a compromise that has only aggravated city problems and caused new ones for suburbanites.

Rather than get a Ph.D. in sociology many bright college graduates are turning their thoughts to earthier matters. They have gone on to composting, organic farming, building fireplaces, horseshoeing and carpentry in an effort to find a really satisfactory life. The protest against war and discrimination in the 1960's emerged into what has been called the "Let's-Live-Decent-Lives" movement of the 1970's.

Certainly some of the new back-to-the-landers are former student protesters and radicals, but not all are. Many are more conservative people, young and old, who simply do not want to live any longer in places they find so basically unpleasant. They are people who value a kind of life that is simply not available in affluent American cities which, despite their lures, cannot offer a life that is quiet and close to earth cycles. The new homesteaders who have departed to look for happiness somewhere else, often are pursuing the image of a pastoral country dream.

The movement from the cities to the country is not something that started in 1970, however, or 1965. In a way it started in the 1930's when many realized that being short of cash is less painful in the country. The movement has continued quietly until the present, and this land rush is merely an increase of degree rather than direction.

Unfortunately for many, the movement back to the land is not based on reality. The vast majority of new homesteaders grew up in cities, have always lived there, and have had little or no experience with farm life. The collectively held image of country life by and large is a myth created by people who do *not* live in the country and who, except for occasional fits of depression, really are fairly satisfied with city living. Country life *can* be idyllic, of course; but it also can be depressing, exhausting and boring. Whatever it is, life in the country is rarely what it seems from a city viewpoint. That is, its values are likely to depend on satisfactions other than those expressed in the dream of a white farmhouse and lilac bushes. What, then, are the realities of rural life? What is modern "homesteading" all about, and what rewards can today's homesteaders possibly expect? To answer these questions, we must backtrack for a moment to consider some historical aspects of homesteading and the immediate predecessors of the modern homestead movement.

## THE HOMESTEAD ACT

In 1862 Congress passed the first Homestead Act to provide a process for the settlement of the vast western lands. Under this law a settler could claim 160 acres of public land, "proving" his claim over a period of five years by clearing and improving his land and living on it for at least six months every year.

The motivation was not altruistic; Congress simply felt that a free land inducement would provide the most equitable settlement of the new territories, preventing the development of huge personal estates, at the same time defending the territories against the Indians.

In the years that followed, millions of acres were settled under the Homestead Act provisions. In time the individual states adopted similar homestead laws for the disposal of state public lands, and in both cases many abuses occurred. The Homestead Law migrations were not isolated events. They were simply part of a general movement to the West that included the periodic opening of new territories seized from the resident Indians.

Life on this frontier was only somewhat more difficult then than life in any rural area. Life was immediate and precarious everywhere. To the problems of drought, flood, cold, providing housing and raising food were added the dangers of "varmints" and Indian attacks.

The singular advantage the homesteaders had in 1862, and throughout the rest of the century, was land, cheap or free for the taking. Their other problems often were severe, but finding a parcel of good land generally was not. Naturally in the older states much of the good land had been taken, as it certainly is today, but there was always land to the west, the reward for the hardships involved in getting there and in getting started.

Since 1862 we have seen the homestead movement ending, the closing of the Western frontier, the movement of farm families to the cities and the rapid growth of technological living. Small holdings have been swallowed by corporate farms, and city dwellers and farmers alike have come to depend utterly on electricity, automobiles, complex machines and appliances, which provide a greatly raised level of physical comfort.

All of these developments followed naturally the rise of industry and the closing of frontiers. It was only natural for many farmers to leave a hard life on the land for the higher wages and shorter hours of industrial work. But time has been able to show us the ultimate consequences of this natural preference for an easier life. Generally speaking the result has been a life for city workers that is less real, has more frustrating working conditions and is far removed from the natural rhythms of the earth.

## PREDECESSORS OF MODERN HOMESTEADING, 1932–1950

For many people the crunch came with the Depression, when well-paid city jobs vanished, and farmers went broke by the thousands. The economic system itself seemed to have gone askew, pinching and pulling nearly everyone. The natural condition seemed to be poverty and confusion.

To re-establish the realities of economic life, Helen and Scott Nearing moved from New York City to Vermont in 1932, achieving what they later called a "saner way to live in a troubled world." They created a small homestead for themselves on a mountain farm, scrupulously avoiding what they felt to be the exploitation of wage-earning and normal consumer buying in the traditional American economy. In 1954 they published their experiences in *Living the Good Life,* which has become a classic account of near-subsistence homesteading. Although their vegetarian austerity was more than many modern homesteaders are willing to accept, many of their practices—paying only by cash or barter, erecting their own buildings from natural materials and developing a small cash product—have become widely accepted in similar subsistence efforts.

The Nearings felt that living in the country, and perhaps taking a step backward in conveniences, was a more reasonable approach to acquiring the real necessities of life. On their homestead they successfully proved the soundness of this viewpoint. For them rural self-sufficiency was the natural counterbalance to widespread economic depression.

A different sort of homesteading approach appeared after the Depression and into World War II, when Ed and Carolyn Robinson started their "productive homestead" in Connecticut. From a typical semi-suburban home the Robinsons developed a detailed "Have-More" plan for raising goats, chickens, cows, a vegetable garden and a small orchard on three acres of land. In 1947, they began publishing and selling booklets, such as "Starting Right with Milk Goats," and "Plan for a Harvest Kitchen." Many of these booklets, dealing with the planning of a country household, its relation to the barn and pastures, and the raising of a few animals, have become classics in the field of country living and still are in print. The Robinsons' message was that country living, even in a relatively urban area, offered *more* satisfactions than city life and provided a *cheaper* way for people to live. Unlike Scott Nearing, though, Ed Robinson kept his city job and pursued homesteading as a creative avocation rather than as a substitute for a regular salary. This is what "homesteading" means today, also, in some definitions.

For the Robinsons and for the Nearings country living was a conscious step. They were greatly concerned with planning their homes and activities, as all homesteaders must be. As city folks they approached rural life with apprehension and excitement, yet with much intelligence. Their aim was not just to survive in the country, but to live *well* there— in fact to live better and to have more than city life seemed to offer.

The Nearings and the Robinsons, of course, are only two families of many who have made the same move and who have chosen and written about country life. Ralph Bordosi's homestead experiments in New Jersey and Peter Dresser's in New Mexico had great effects on the back-to-the-land movement. The Nearings and Robinsons are mentioned here simply because their experiences seem so representative and the quality of their writing so high. They also embraced the whole range of modern country living—from the carefully economical and self-sufficient vegetarian life to a more suburban, part-time homestead.

Despite the examples provided by these homestead people, the movement of Americans *to* the cities continued to the present, though it was countered by a trickle of "eccentrics" back to the land. Today that trickle has become a flood, as thousands flee the metropolitan areas every year. Subsistence homesteading once was the province of the pioneer, then the eccentric individualist, then the hippie dropout. Today it is the province of many very average people who want a healthy, alternative life. The resource and energy crisis which loomed in 1973 certainly has speeded this trend.

To get back to our earlier question, the motivation of homesteaders is clearly to get away from economic exploitation and the prime need for cash and material things that exist in any urban life. But exactly what are homesteaders getting away *to?* What rewards can modern homesteaders expect? What exactly constitutes a homestead?

HOMESTEADING TODAY

The wide range of lifestyles that are lumped under "homesteading" makes a precise definition difficult. Even so, there are a few basic features without which a country home could not be called a homestead at all. They are:

> *A piece of land,* probably between 2 and 50 acres, and usually owned by the homesteader.

*A garden,* by which the homesteader provides a large part of his food.

An effort toward *self-sufficiency,* usually involving the reduction of cash needs, the development of a cash income other than full-time employment, and the raising or making of some home products.

Of course homesteads differ as much as their owners. Some raise beef cattle, some are vegetarians; some use a cash crop like maple syrup to buy much of their food, others buy almost nothing from outside stores. Some homesteaders, like Helen and Scott Nearing, live very careful lives and have lively intellectual interests; others create sprawling farmsteads and feast on evenings of television.

Perhaps one other generalization might be ventured. By and large, the demands of this life mean that most homesteaders are intelligent, practical and adventurous people who give top value to their freedom and independence. They know how to plan well ahead for efficient living, how to discipline themselves to the tasks at hand, and how to invent homemade solutions to mechanical problems. Especially homesteaders are people who genuinely enjoy living in the country and do not particularly miss the man-created aspects of urban life.

It probably would be safe to say that successful homesteaders today are fairly serious people, not given to flippant whims or frolics. They know that survival on the land is a serious matter.

As we shall see, the nature of homesteading requires such traits as frugality and a capacity for sustained hard work. These traits develop necessarily as part of running a successful homestead, and are probably not indigenous to potential homesteaders.

Homesteaders can be young or old (Scott Nearing was 49 when he moved to Vermont), but the more self-sufficient the homestead the more apt they are to be young. If much is made of homesteaders with graduate degrees, it is precisely because a degree is so eminently useless to a homesteader. While a reasonable amount of native intelligence is needful, just as special skills like carpentry, drafting or bricklaying are useful, a fine education doesn't necessarily help.

All the same, we often see Ph.D. candidates on the homestead, as well as men and women who could, and often did, have brilliant careers in all sorts of city professions. What do they find that is so attractive? What does rural homesteading offer them that urban society cannot?

REWARDS OF HOMESTEADING

1. *Independence.* First and most important homesteading offers a certain kind of real independence. Americans have always been unimpressed with domination by others, whether politically or economically, for most would like to be their own bosses. An ornery fondness for personal independence keeps cropping up, whether in folklore or real life. To a degree the homesteader's independence is psychological, but there are tangible sides to it as well.

For people who enjoy good food, good in taste and nutrition, homesteading is an actual alternative to consumer living. Instead of buying your eggs at a supermarket you gather them from your henhouse. Instead of buying milk and vegetables, you milk the cow or goat and harvest your garden. Instead of buying cheese and butter, you make your own.

The independent homesteader enjoys a certain security, too. City dwellers are well acquainted with the consequences of garbage strikes, blackouts, runaway prices, scarce goods and unsafe neighborhoods. A homesteader is not nearly so vulnerable nor so easily inconvenienced. He is protected by having his own food supply, his own sanitation system and his "backup systems" of kerosene lamps and wood-burning stoves. Some have their own generating systems; others don't even use electricity. The homesteader need not depend much on others.

Financially the homesteader has a larger degree of independence from banks and insurance companies. There is a reduced need to have costly insurance on a home he built for $900 in one month, and theft insurance in most places is unnecessary. Many homesteaders also are able to buy their own land outright and construct a house for a relatively low cost, thereby escaping the all-pervasive mortgage, when it can be secured from lending institutions. If a homesteader does make a monthly payment, it is going toward his own land title, not as rent to a landlord. Reducing one's debts and financial needs is a welcome part of homesteading, another step toward independence.

Finally, the homesteader is independent in the best sense from the frustrations of traffic, waiting lines, delays, construction din, factory pollution, and, if he locates intelligently, the ever-creeping strip development along suburban roadsides. Many urbanites may shrink at the prospect of "empty" evenings and totally silent nights, but homesteaders come to enjoy relying on themselves for entertainment. Since living in the country suggests following nature's rhythms, it is an unusual night that a country dweller stays up many hours after dark anyway.

2. *Living in harmony with nature.* The homesteader's house-building usually is accomplished in spring or summer, as in the following years are normal preparations for winter—the cutting of firewood, starting the garden, composting and cutting hay. The seasons and the weather rule farm or homestead life.

The wise homesteader thinks ahead seasonally, even as he works from day to day. He learns the days and seasons for action, and the times for waiting. One might say that homesteading teaches him to compost not only the garden, but his own life—to digest and learn from mistakes, to ripen toward new opportunities. It teaches him to work with the conditions of the earth and to pay attention to the sun, rain and wind.

3. *Practical creativity.* For this, one could also write self-reliance, since both involve a satisfaction in personal accomplishment. Building your house with your own hands is *creatively* satisfying. So are growing beans, raising chickens or nursing a sick animal back to health, inventing your children's playthings, devising a helpful household tool, converting an abandoned shed into something useful—the list of practical satisfactions on a homestead is a long one. A homesteader's creativity is more apt to be expressed in his daily work than in formal art forms, but it is no less satisfying—perhaps is more so. For what a homesteader creates is the ultimate art form—his own world.

Part of the satisfaction of homestead inventiveness is learning to be resourceful—acquiring a new understanding for what is actually useful, and a new frugality about making do instead of buying. It also may in-

volve becoming a jack-of-all-trades to bring in extra cash income toward paying necessary cash expenses.

The motivations of homesteaders seem to revolve around the single idea of *bringing together cause and effect.* People who homestead are trying to reduce the long chain of technological society to a few short links. You plant a seed and get a carrot. You cut some trees and use them to build a house. This idea is in direct opposition to advanced industrial society, where you work at a job (possibly boring) to earn money that you trade for a commercially-grown carrot that may have come from 2000 miles away. In bringing cause and effect together, other things also seem to come together for homesteaders almost automatically. There is something inherently satisfying about the physical and mental labor—perhaps akin to the intense pleasure that small boys have in building forts and tree houses. Because they build for themselves, homesteaders I have talked to generally have been aggressively happy.

## THE REALITIES OF HOMESTEADING

Although the motivations of homesteaders are appealing, the rewards and the happiness derived constitute only one side of the picture. They are like the country fantasy we carry around with us—sometimes true but not totally accurate. For there are painful sides to homesteading. Every year many people move to the land and then fail or give up in disgust. They get rained out, have accidents, make strategic errors, run out of money or don't like the life. Homesteading simply is not for everyone. There are plenty of hard facts that should be examined by anyone who wants to have a realistic picture of what his move back to the land would be like.

Here is a list of basic features of homesteading that must be considered by anyone planning this way of life. They will be discussed at greater length in the chapters that follow.

1. *Land.* Real estate brokers have a favorite quote: "Under all is the land," and this is more important to consider in homesteading than any-

where else. The first step in starting a homestead is to locate and buy suitable land. Not just any old place will do for a house, but land that has good water, a fertile garden area and perhaps a necessary woodlot or pasture. Having good land, in the right climate and location, is absolutely essential for this long-term, earthy enterprise to succeed.

Many people start out on the wrong foot by buying more land than they can afford or by failing to make sure that the land will meet their needs. Such mistakes sometimes can be corrected, as poor soil gradually can be built up to a reasonable level of fertility. Even so, buying land is a delicate step, to be undertaken carefully. You will enjoy (or suffer) your land for years afterward.

2. *Shelter.* If the land you buy has no building on it, you must construct the shelter you need—something suitable to the climate, your family, animals and equipment. Simply doing this will require many skills that may be new to you. Again, the opportunity to make mistakes is great, and such mistakes can be too costly for you to sustain.

While it need not be very expensive, your shelter is something you must plan for when deciding how much to spend for land. Remember, also, your house probably will cost about double what you anticipate. And don't forget the time factors. Much of homesteading consists of work on shelters of various kinds, especially in the beginning.

3. *Food.* For homesteaders having a food supply isn't quite as simple as taking dollars down to the corner market; and you will have other needs for the dollars, besides. You will want to grow your own vegetables and perhaps raise milk or meat animals. This involves setting out a garden, tending it, harvesting, and preserving as much as you can for winter use. Having animals means learning how to care for them and doing it month in and month out. It means buying and growing animal feed, milking twice a day and paying veterinary bills.

There are important rewards in having animals and a large garden, but the work is there all the same. What you gain in reduced grocery bills, you exchange for time and physical effort.

4. *Money.* Getting back to the land, unfortunately, isn't the end of your need for money. In some ways it is only the beginning. Initially homesteading can be a surprisingly expensive proposition, for like any new business venture it takes adequate starting capital. Land must be bought, often for thousands of dollars. Building materials, tools, vehicles,

animals, grain and seeds must be paid for. On a continuing basis taxes must be paid, vehicles maintained, and doctors' bills met.

New homesteaders also sometimes overlook the need for a steady cash income *after* the homestead is established. In the glow of early enthusiasm such petty matters may seem unimportant. But ongoing expenses can make the going mighty rough if they come as a surprise. A wise homesteader not only will have reasonable savings, but will have a planned and sure source of regular income for the future.

5. *Planning.* A successful, smoothly running homestead depends more than anything else upon planning ahead. Planning starts when you look at a piece of land and begin to think about financing—and it never ends. Income and expenses must be planned, houses must be planned, gardens must be planned. To keep warm in winter you plan to cut firewood the previous year. To have a garden in the spring, you plan composting in the summer and fall.

A homesteader must decide in advance what work must be done and when—and he must *do* the work according to the plans he has made. Perhaps for the first time he must be his own and very exacting boss. Lack of logical planning and follow-through probably are the biggest factors when a homesteading venture fails. Their importance cannot be overemphasized.

6. *Hard work.* Hard work, both on and off the homestead, is an inescapable part of this life. Much physical work and long hours are required, of course—for things such as carpentry, tree-felling, digging pipelines, hauling hay or manure, splitting wood or building fences. There also is the mental work of keeping records, drawing up accounts, studying agricultural pamphlets and working out building plans. In addition, if you work outside for cash, there is the getting to the job and putting in your hours there, whatever you may be doing. Living on the land should be satisfying, but it is not an easy life, especially not physically. Don't forget that farmers often work a 16-hour day that starts at 5 a.m. You may be doing the same, at least for a while.

7. *Social life.* One of the undeniable conditions of the country, especially on a homestead, is its difference from the city's social life. Here friends drop in or neighbors get together in town occasionally, but for the most part homesteading is a solitary life. A family or couple on a homestead may feel (and be) quite isolated; they may miss the fun or

frequent parties or meetings and many friends. A family is thrown upon itself for nearly all its day-to-day companionship, especially in winter when neighborly visits are few and far between.

Despite the benefits of being busy, this increased dependence on each other can become a real problem if a family member had reservations about the move in the first place. Marriage strains will grow, feeding on the hard work involved simply in establishing the homestead. Sometimes the strain is too much, and the marriage as well as the homestead goes down the drain. The best preparation is to be certain that homesteading is the life you *both* want—otherwise it probably will destroy a shaky marriage.

Of course there *are* social pleasures in country living, and eventually you may find that your rural friends are the best you've ever had. Neighbors, too, usually turn out to be friendly and helpful—more so in the country. But until such ties are established you must be able to live alone and like it.

Homesteading, then, is not the answer to all urban problems, any more than it is a life that appeals to everyone. As I have tried to show, much hard work is involved; it demands great practicality, a disinterest in having much money, and the stamina to endure bad weather and hard times. Whether the pleasures outweigh the pains depends on you.

### HOW TO TELL IF HOMESTEADING IS FOR YOU

1. *Try to look at yourself objectively.* If you grew up in Paramus, New Jersey and have had no experience with country living, ask yourself: *Why do I want to leave the kind of life I am living? What am I really looking for in the country?* Make a list of the rewards you expect. Especially, tote up *what talents or interests you have that you think will enable you to live happily in the new and foreign environment.*

Answering difficult questions like these (and others discussed later) is important, and doing so early in your thinking may save you misery and money later on. Many city people *do* need a change or a move, but they don't necessarily need to move to rural Maine or British Columbia. If, on the one hand, yours is not a country background (and most people's isn't), you will have much to learn, and to give up. You have, in other words, every reason to assume that you would *not* be happy as a homesteader. After all, there are other, less drastic modes of country life.

On the other hand, you may discover you are genuinely frustrated by *not* being a homesteader (which you probably knew long ago). In any case, take a very long look at your motives. Look at your skills, your ability with tools, your preferences for entertainment, and your opinion on weeding gardens. The best time for having second thoughts is while you're still contemplating the trade-in value of your green Cadillac, *not* after you've bought ten swampy acres of cutover forest in Michigan.

2. *Read about homesteading and rural living.* Read everything you can find about buying land, raising rabbits and goats, building log cabins or rigging a windmill. Learn to read between the lines. Don't be taken in by overly-romantic accounts of how the Allbottoms enjoy perfect health and happiness raising organic food in the Ozarks. Homesteading is never a picnic, so be wary of books and magazines that make country living sound like paradise, especially in California and the Southwest.

Look for realistic personal accounts of homestead life, preferably those written by those who seem to share your values and viewpoint. Read the Nearings' *Living The Good Life* and Ed Robinson's "Have-More Plan." (See chapter appendix.)

3. *Write to homesteaders.* Periodicals, such as *The Mother Earth News* and *Countryside* (see Chapter Seven appendix) run letters and ads from people who are homesteading or would like to be. Place an ad yourself or write to likely-sounding advertisers, explaining your plans or hopes, and ask for their advice or thoughts. Some will be too busy to reply, but others will be glad to share their experiences with you. You may end up as long-term friends, especially if you settle in their area.

4. *Visit a homestead.* If your correspondent sounds promising, arrange to visit his farm or homestead for a few days. Share in the work and entertainment, such as it may be. If you can't arrange a visit by using the magazines mentioned above, place an ad in a rural newspaper or visit an area that attracts you. Explain your mission to a local real estate broker or postmaster, either of whom may be able to suggest a farmstead where you might be welcome.

A visit to a homestead is the very best way to find out your fitness for homestead life. You may feel like a foreigner at first, but as the days pass you should begin to feel comfortable with the country routine and be able to make your contribution to the work. You will soon know whether your own thoughts about homesteading are in tune with your abilities and with things as they are.

5. *Urban homesteading.* Homesteading is not only a country thing, but also is possible in some cities. In Wilmington, Delaware and Philadelphia, for instance, urban homesteaders can now "buy" a condemned urban renewal area house for $1, renovate it, and receive title to the house after five years of "proving" their claim—much like the old homesteaders.

Programs of financial help and construction review are being set up to help homesteaders get loans and meet city building codes. Even though the renovation cost may be $10-15,000, there aren't nearly enough old houses for all the people who want to try this alternative to a conventional house buy. Other cities are watching these experiments with much interest, and city homesteaders may be one of the new solutions to urban problems.


This chapter has emphasized not the pleasures and rewards of homesteading, but the hard work and care required in beginning this kind of country life. The reason is this: It is very easy to drive through the country and find the white farmhouse and red barn that seem the epitome of country life. It is far better to realize that this quaint country place likely has no plumbing, no central heating, has sagging floors and rotted sills, poor insulation, and a damp cellar. It is likely to have no adequate water supply. The land around it may be eroded or pocked with rusty farm machinery hidden in the weeds. Out back may be a rotted and sagging barn and the remains of an old fruit orchard. This bleak picture probably is an exaggeration, but it is no more extreme than the idyllic version we often imagine. The truth may lie somewhere between.

To succeed, potential homesteaders must recognize and accept the realities of country or backwoods life—the isolation, hard work, necessity for planning and practical skills—and the need for cash. From what I know and have seen, the homesteaders who turn out happy are those who are able to enjoy the work and derive their pleasures from accomplishing what they set out to do. They are happy because they have *chosen* the pleasures and the pains of a simple life, along with its "days of solid satisfaction."

# APPENDIX

## SUGGESTED READING

> NOTE: *Books listed in this and the following bibliographies with no price were out of print in 1974 but may be found in many public libraries. Paperback editions are listed when available.*

Angier, Bradford
>One Acre and Security. New York, Random House, 1972. 319 pp. $2.45 paperback.

Bordosi, Ralph
>Flight from the City: An Experiment in Creative Living on the Land. New York, Harper & Row, 1972. $1.95 paperback.

Gourlie, John
>How to Locate in the Country. Charlotte, VT, Garden Way, 1973. 97 pp. $2.50 paperback.

Gustafson, A. F.; Hardenburg, E. V.; Smith, E. Y.; McCay, Jeanette
>Land for the Family, A Guide to Country Living. Ithaca, Comstock Publishing, 1947. 501 pp. hardback.

Houriet, Robert
>Getting Back Together. New York, Coward-McCann, 1971. 408 pp. $1.25 paperback (Avon).

Kains, M. G.
>Five Acres and Independence. New York, Dover Publications, 1935 and 1973. $2.50 paperback.

Kaysing, William
>How to Live in the New America. Englewood Cliffs, NJ, Prentice-Hall, 1973. 56 pp. $8.95 hardback.

Lappe, Francis Moore
>Diet for a Small Planet. New York, Ballantine, 1971. 300 pp. $1.25 paperback.

Nearing, Helen & Scott
>Living the Good Life. New York, Schocken Books, 1954. 213 pp. $4.95 hardback; $1.95 paperback.

Robinson, Ed & Carolyn
   The "Have-More" Plan. Charlotte, VT, Garden Way, 1943. 82 pp. $2.50
   paperback.

CHAPTER TWO
# BUYING LAND

As a beginning homesteader your first and most critical move will be to buy a piece of land. You should proceed carefully in your choice, considering the region, the state or geographic area, and the community that you want. When you have reached the point of looking at specific parcels of land, you will want to make sure that the land suits your basic needs. Although past experience is helpful, keeping a clear head and deciding in advance *specifically* what you are looking for will keep you from making a foolish purchase, even if you are new at this. Because your land will be your first big homestead expense, proceed systematically in buying what you need. Ultimately, much of your happiness and success will depend on the land you choose.

## HOMESTEAD (PUBLIC) LAND

Today there is very little land available for genuine homesteading in the original sense. Most public lands to be had in the continental United States are barren semi-desert in .such states as Nevada or Utah. Some is also available in Alaska. This land is sold at public auctions by the Bureau of Land Management, either through sealed or oral bidding. For information on available public land, write to the BLM (see chapter appendix) for its quarterly, "Our Public Lands," which lists land to be sold in the near future.

Land can also be purchased under the "General Mining Laws" established by Congress in 1872. These provide that you may claim up to 20 acres by finding a mineral on the land and doing a certain amount of work on your claim each year. For further information, write to the BLM for a copy of the General Mining Laws and their free booklet, "Patenting a Mining Claim on Federal Lands."

Other public land can be leased through the Bureau of Reclamation, which develops irrigation or power projects. Information on lease lands can be obtained from the Department of the Interior, Bureau of Reclamation (see chapter appendix).

Finally, public land is available for sale through the General Service Administration, which is responsible for disposing of "surplus" federal property. For information about scheduled sales, write to the U.S. Government Printing Office (see chapter appendix) for listings in "Commerce Business Daily," or to the General Services Administration. For details of how to proceed in buying public land, write for *Locating and Buying Low Cost Land,* Wallin Publications (see chapter appendix). It gives much useful advice about land auctions and conditions.

Buying government land can be a cheap way to find what you want; except that you will have to put up with miles of red tape over many months. In the end, however, you may be able to buy marginal land at a fraction of what you would pay for similar land bought privately.

CHOOSING AN AREA

Everyone has his own idea of the kind of place where he would like to live. Some prefer a warm climate the year around; others feel restless without lots of snow in winter. When you choose a homestead area you naturally will take these preferences into account. If you like snow and happen to have relatives in Minnesota, it is a natural place to consider. On the other hand, you may want to stay far away from your Minnesota relatives. In either instance, you have definite reasons for narrowing your search.

The choice of a *general area* in which to look for land is largely personal: the presence of friends, some knowledge of the area or even an unfulfilled childhood longing. Also different states within the same region have a different "feel" to them. Only you can decide where you will be most comfortable.

The climate may well affect your search. One hundred inches of rain every spring or seven inches of rain all year—these factors will appall or appeal. But remember that 40 inches a year is ideal for gardening. Even if you do not know right away where you would like to live, careful evaluations in time will lead to the place you've been looking for.


## EVALUATING A COMMUNITY

Once you have decided on the general region or area that you like, look carefully at the individual communities. There are many factors that will determine your final choice, such as the availability of jobs, schools, cultural centers, or markets for your skills. *How to Locate in the Country,* by John Gourlie (see Chapter One appendix), explains the importance of the surrounding countryside and gives detailed checklists for evaluating your prospective community. Following are some of Mr. Gourlie's most important factors:

1. *Community spirit.* Probably the best indication of the quality of a community is how the residents feel about it. Do they take pride in their area? Are they friendly and helpful to newcomers? Are community organizations active and enthusiastic? Are the homes kept up well? If the answer to any of these questions is no, you may not want to live there. Of course, taciturn natives don't always open up to visitors, especially in places like New England, but you should be able to sense the community spirit—or lack of it.

2. *Homesteaders.* Are there other homesteaders or similar people in the area? If so, you can get a good picture of the community by talking to them. If there is none, there may be a good reason for it. You might have a hard time being accepted, even if the other factors were suitable for homesteading.

3. *Schools and medical facilities.* In your quest for rural isolation don't overlook the need for schools for your children and medical facilities for all of you. Schools and a hospital should not be too far away and the

quality should be good. Along the same line, be sure there is a veterinarian available for your animals if you expect to have any.

4. *Job opportunities*. Being able to earn a cash income is very important, especially during the first few years. Your choice of a community may well depend on what jobs are available to match the skills you have. Also, consider travel time to possible jobs. You may wish to locate within reasonable traveling distance of a town.

5. *Transportation*. Besides distances, consider the difficulty of winter travel. A more expensive place on a paved or good dirt road may be a better buy than one that is frequently snowed or mudded in. What is the public transit situation? Bear in mind how much you want to spend on transportation both in time and money.

6. *Social life*. You already may be willing to do without a lot of city entertainments, but you must know what kind of social life you *do* need, and what's available. Cheaper land in the backwoods may be too expensive for you in terms of isolation, and you would be happier paying a little more to be closer to town.

If you follow the John Gourlie checklist, you will see that there are many considerations in choosing a homestead area. Some of the items may seem farfetched or trivial at first; only you can determine what is important. Nevertheless, finding the *right* land involves more than just finding suitable land. Don't overlook the need for social services and community relations, good friends, good neighbors, necessary facilities and a job market.

LOCATING LAND FOR SALE

Once you decide on a limited area, you can begin to explore specific paths to securing the right piece of land. Occasionally a perfect opportunity will fall into your lap, but generally the following methods are the most productive:

1. *Land sale agencies*. There are several companies that deal in nationwide land sales and publish periodic catalogs. The best-known are *Strout Realty* and *United Farm Agency* (see chapter appendix). Their catalogs are free, and in almost every area they have affiliated realtors who will show you the land listed in the regional catalog. These well-established

companies have brought many people to the land they were looking for. Of course there may be many other local agencies in your chosen area, too. But these national companies are a good start, especially in getting a feel for current land prices in a relatively unfamiliar area.

Other prominent firms are the *Safebuy Agency* and *The Link,* which publishes eastern and western editions (see chapter appendix). *The Link* has fewer listings, and unlike Strout Realty, it does not offer pictures of its properties.

2. *Personal visits.* The very best way to find a piece of land is to visit an area you like. Perhaps you have friends or spend vacations or summers there. At any rate, travel around on the back roads. If you have time, get to know the local residents—go to local affairs, auctions, meetings. Get a feel for the area, the people and the land market. There may be a land boom going on, but you may not realize it, without questions, until you have wasted a few weeks looking around.

3. *Realtors.* Unless you have lived in an area for quite a while (and perhaps even if you have), you'll want to check with local real estate people. In dealing with them, you have nothing to lose and everything to gain, assuming that you know what you want and aren't easily talked into a bad buy. Realtors know the local land market better than you ever could. They can produce from their files in minutes several suitable places that might take you weeks of personal investigation to uncover.

The real estate broker's fee usually is paid by the seller, so it doesn't cost you anything to work through him. At the same time let him work for you. The real estate man has more than a file of properties for sale, however. If he is a good one he has years of experience listing and selling in that area. He will know the history of nearly every piece of property in town: the present owner, the past owners, what's wrong (or right) with it and its present market value. He also probably knows the owner personally, and perhaps how much he'll come down from his asking price. Finally, the broker knows the local development trends—the tax rate, areas where land costs are inflated, and the local attitudes in the community about newcomers.

In dealing with a broker be honest and specific. As an incipient homesteader, you should have a good idea of what you want—perhaps not as precise an idea as a farmer would have, but certainly better than a young couple out for a Sunday drive who fancy someday finding a country home.

If you need 20 acres and can't afford $1000 an acre, say so. The agent may shake his head and tell you that there's nothing available, but at least you haven't wasted your time or his. If you are looking for a rundown farm or a small old house, say so. There's no sense in chasing around looking at retirement homes or expensive views.

An agent wants to sell you a place, however, and the less time he spends at it, the higher his profit. He may try to hurry you from one place to another or suggest that you're hard to please. No matter. It's your money you are spending, so don't be hurried. No matter what else you do in buying land, take your time. And ask plenty of questions. For me the best advice is this: *know what you want, be honest and take your time.* You are under no obligation for anything until you actually sign a purchase agreement.

4. *Other sources of land.* Besides using local real estate brokers, there are other ways to locate land for sale. One is the local newspaper, which will carry personal as well as Realtors' listings. Even if it does not have what you want, the paper is a good way to find out about the area: local interests, political struggles, store prices, social events and the specific neighborhood characteristics.

Another good source, especially if you have lived in the area for a while, is the grapevine. Through your friends you may hear of someone who would like to sell his land, well before he gets around to listing or advertising it. Many people, in fact, quietly ask for buyers among their acquaintances before they consider a public listing. You even may find that actively asking around of land for sale will prompt someone to sell who had no real intention to do so. People like to know who their neighbors are going to be. If they like you, they may go out of their way to help find what you want.


HOW MUCH LAND TO BUY

Many would-be homesteaders start out thinking that they need 50 to 100 acres. Their rationale is usually that they want plenty of space to ride horses, or they want to keep neighbors at a distance. Sometimes they are thinking of a large farm, even though they do not plan to run a farm as such.

Generally it is a mistake to buy too much land, for several reasons. For one thing land requires maintenance and use or it "goes to seed," growing up with weeds, brush or small trees. For another, land costs money and carries annual tax assessments. True, land values always increase, but capital gains are not what you're after. Buying more than you need ties up your savings unnecessarily and adds to your annual cash costs. Unless you can easily afford to keep your land idle and pay these extra costs, you are better off to buy only what you will need for your homestead.

It's impossible to specify how large a homestead should be, but most people would not need more than a few acres, perhaps fifteen at the outside. It is perfectly possible to have a lovely and fairly self-sufficient homestead on five acres, provided it is all good land.

To illustrate, here is a suggested layout for a 4-acre homestead that appeared in Ed Robinson's "Have-More" Plan. He described it as follows:

> These four acres of good land would not only provide the family vegetables, fruit, and berries, but more than enough pasture and hay for two or three milk goats or pasture for a cow and a good part of a cow's hay requirements. There is also room for a pig or two plus other livestock.

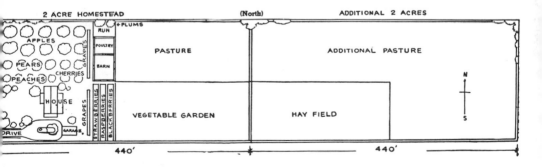

As you can see from the layout, the front two acres could easily stand alone, especially if you had a single milk goat. You'd still have the fruit trees, garden, berries and poultry shed.

Even if you do not expect to be as well-organized and efficient as Ed and Carolyn Robinson you probably do not need as much land as you think. Unless you plan to have a working farm and have had farming experience, you are better off to plan on a small homestead.

The one exception to this rule is the purchase of a woodlot if you plan to heat with wood. Wood stoves and a five-acre woodlot growing good fuel wood will save you money, and the woodland may well be priced lower per acre than your open homestead land. (See Chapter Six for a more detailed discussion of woodlots and wood heating.)

### TIME CONSIDERATIONS

The time of year is important in buying land. On a beautiful spring day the whole world looks lovely, and you might agree to a purchase you later regret. As a general rule try to look at land during the off seasons—late fall, winter or very early spring. Not only will you see everything at its worst, which is what you want, but the broker will be less hurried and will have more time to show you various places. If you are forced to look for land in the spring or summer, make a similar effort to go on a cloudy or rainy day. In selecting a time to look, take into account, also, your own internal rhythms. After a long winter or a particularly bad experience in the city you may be a sucker for any small farm.

## EVALUATING YOUR LAND

As you visit and inspect various pieces of land you may be trying to remember all that you need to check, but your head will be whirling with half-remembered guidelines. Even if you have a clear idea of what you are looking for, the excitement of actually going through an old house or walking around the back field may distract you from more important features. Here, then, is a list to keep in mind and make notes on as you look at homestead lands.

1. *Fertility.* The fertility of house lots in Levittown is not too critical. For a homestead, however, the quality of the soil is primary, for much of your food savings will depend on having good soil. Scoop some up in your fingers. Does it harden into a lump of mud? It may have too much clay content. Is it too sandy? Or does it remain light and crumbly? This is one indication that it is good soil.

Look at the plants already on the property. Are they healthy and lush? Are there plenty of dark green, sturdy weeds? If so, the land is probably good. If the weeds are scraggly and thin the soil probably is too poor to support a garden.

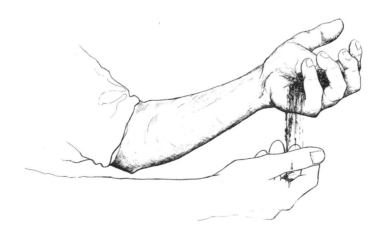

Look also at the trees. If you have beech, maple or oak the soil probably is good. If you see scrub pine or stunted trees, the soil is poor. Willow, poplar and alder indicate that the soil is too wet.

Have a sample of the soil tested at your state or county agricultural office. It's done free or for a nominal charge. When you gather soil for testing also be sure to test the depth of topsoil. If it is too thin, you may have trouble with erosion and shallow roots. If your topsoil rests on hardpan or bedrock, you'll have trouble with drainage, your waste system and excavation for a cellar.

An excellent source of information about soil quality by area is the United States Department of Agriculture, which has compiled soil maps for much of the United States. These maps, which are available at your county agricultural office, show patterns of soil quality as a topographic map shows terrain. But there are local variations which make soil sample tests important.

2. *Location.* The highest-priced property today is waterfront land or land with a view. It may be on a hilltop or halfway up a mountain. The people who demand a good view usually are building vacation homes and are notoriously impractical.

The best location for a homestead, assuming good soil and water, is on a gentle slope, neither in the valley nor on a hilltop, for the slope will provide good drainage. Living in a valley increases the risk of flood damage, a wet basement and heavy frosts. Although the view may be lovely, a hilltop house is exposed to winter winds, is expensive to heat and implies a hill to climb. If you can find a logical homesite with a view, that is fine, but there are more important considerations. Look for southern exposures and protection from prevailing winds.

3. *Water.* Water is essential on any homestead, so check carefully for springs or existing wells. If you are lucky, you will find a year-round spring on a slope above your chosen house site. This is a wonderful situation, since you need only install a gravity pipeline to your house. Next best is a good spring nearby, from which you can pump water. Make sure somebody else doesn't own the spring rights.

If there's no spring you may have to drill for water, an undertaking that can cost $1500 or more for a deep well, if it's required. Many people have had to drill for water after buying property which they thought had

a good spring. They failed to inspect it in late summer when many springs go dry.

When visiting possible land buys be sure to take a sterile bottle water sample and have it tested for purity. If there is no ready source of water, ask a near neighbor about the depth of his well. His answers will give you some idea what to expect on the land you are considering.

A final part of water quality is *hardness*. Hard water builds up deposits inside water pipes, sometimes to the point of stopping the flow, and causing you, the victim, the trouble of digging up the pipes and replacing them. Stories come to mind of pioneer women traveling with a bar of soap and finally selecting a homestead for its soft water. Though it is a minor worry, you should keep it in mind.

4. *Drainage.* When you inspect any piece of land keep an eye open for drainage. Problems may come up later, if your septic tank starts contaminating your well, for example. But even in the beginning make sure that the surface water drains somewhere besides your favored house site. If the soil is very clayey, think twice. Clay holds water and may cause a septic system to back up if the water table is too high. It's unstable to build on, too. Your drainage is probably all right as long as the soil is good and the slope of the land is apparent.

5. *Woods.* The ideal homestead would be partly wooded, with enough

open land and fairly even ground for a house, garden and pastures. Most homesteaders in the northern states heat with wood, so a woodlot is quite necessary. The alternative is to buy or scavenge fuel wood.

Sometimes land is available that either is completely wooded or has been "clear cut," which means that everything of useful size has been cut off. In either instance you will be able to buy the land more cheaply. However, clearing land is expensive and time-consuming. It may eventually cost you more, in years lost getting your homestead under way. It is almost always better, if possible, to buy land that is already partly clear.

Clear-cut land has other disadvantages. Besides having to remove stumps and small trees, you will not have the large trees for firewood and fences that you'll need. You still will have the work of clearing part of your land after the lumber company has taken the useful trees. There might be some circumstances, such as a very low price, that would make this purchase attractive, but be especially wary of this kind of "bargain" land. It isn't often a good buy.

A final note on woodlots: While a small woodlot (five to ten acres) may be important for supplying firewood (if it's good burning wood), a large number of wooded acres (fifty or more) is not necessarily a wise purchase. The argument is sometimes made that the lumber you can harvest will make the woodlot pay for itself. However, this often is not true. Your best move, if you are considering the purchase of a largely wooded homestead, is to have the trees inspected by a professional or county forester, who can give you an estimate of their value. Weigh the possible forest yield per year against the land's taxes.

6. *Access.* Parcels of land sometimes are available cheaply because they have no road frontage or access, such as a farmer's back field. Such a purchase may be a good buy, *if* there is an established and deeded access road on the property. If there is not, you have a serious problem. Incredible as it sounds, people do buy land, of course without realizing it, that they can't legally get to. The only thing to do then is to pay the neighbor-owner whatever he asks for a right-of-way.

If your land has no road frontage, but does have a deeded right-of-way, you still may have a problem with the costs of building and maintaining your private driveway. Generally it is a good idea to be cautious about land any distance off a public road. If it is, make sure that there is a right-

of-way (not a public one, either) and insist that it be spelled out in the purchase contract.

7. *Price and other costs.* Although more will be said about land costs in the next section, there are two cost factors to consider immediately. First, be wary of any land that is selling at a very low price or land that is out of line with similar parcels in the area. Find out what the going price for land is in the area and then expect to pay it. A very low price should alert you to real problems or a deception.

Second, find out from the county or town clerk what you can expect to pay for taxes. This is a routine matter, but it should not be overlooked. Taxes are an inescapable part of owning land, and they will be one of your regular cash expenses in the years that follow.

8. *Zoning and building codes.* Before making up your mind about a piece of land, check into the local zoning regulations and applicable building codes. Some rural areas have neither, but it is wise to be sure. It might turn out that the land is ideal, but that you would not be allowed to erect the sort of buildings you wanted or to set up certain types of businesses or keep animals. This kind of regulation would be quite likely in an area that is becoming suburban. On the other hand, zoning which precluded industrial development near you would be valuable.

9. *Use of old buildings.* Even if you plan to build your own house, take the trouble to look at a few pieces of land with buildings on them. Unless you plan to commute to your land while you build, or camp out, you may find an old, barely livable house already on the place will be very useful. Remember, too, that buying a place with a shelter, even if temporary, will allow you to turn your immediate attention to other aspects of setting up your homestead, such as animal barns, garden, cutting wood, fixing the water supply, and so on.

A word of caution, though, if you buy an old house with the idea of renovating it. Unless remarkably sound, it often will cost as much to renovate as it would to build afresh. If you prefer to renovate anyway, keep in mind that you will not necessarily save money.

10. *Title search.* Finally, have a local attorney search the title (or do it yourself if you know how). Make sure that the present owner has a clear title and that there are no old rights-of-way or easements or liens on the property unknowingly carried along. Such possibilities are almost endless: neighbors who have a legal right to drive their cows to pasture across

your intended garden site; farmers who own water or grazing rights where you wish to have your chickens. Especially important, as I have mentioned, is your exclusive right of access. A title search should un- cover any previous rights that have been granted or retained by previous owners. If such rights exist and are limiting to your use of the property, you will have to buy exclusive rights from the holders, or give up the plan to buy.

## LAND COSTS

Today there is a land boom going on almost everywhere in the United States. Rural land values in particular have zoomed out of sight in the last ten years. In Maine, for instance, land which sold at $15 an acre three years ago sells today for $250—the same land, no improvements. And this is land that has no road frontage. In British Columbia land values have risen to $2000 an acre in some rural areas, and the price is even higher in towns or near developed areas. Taxes go up with values, and as a consequence many farmers are forced to sell their land because of rising taxes. Farmland then is bought by developers or speculators and resold— sometimes as "homesteads"—at a fabulous profit. This boom is expected to continue.

Land is not cheap anywhere anymore. Even in Alaska, where people suppose there are thousands of acres of open land, prices are high. Be prepared to pay for your land probably more than you would like or expect.

But there is one bright side to this situation, and it is this: *Some land is cheaper than other land.* For instance, it is much cheaper to buy land in upstate New York, northern New Hampshire or West Virginia than it is anywhere in Connecticut. You may be able to find good land here for as little as $100 or $200 an acre, though it will take some hard looking.

The demand for country land is like any other demand. Some places are more popular than others. As you get away from the cities, from the quaint little town and from the resorts, land costs decrease. If you can find a place so remote that absolutely nobody else wants to live there, you prob- ably can get land very, very cheaply. However, you will probably find that there is a certain point of isolation beyond which you are unwilling to go. At that point you must be willing to pay the market value for what you want.

The best time to buy land, other than ten years ago, is *now*. If you know what kind of land you want and how much land you need, you still can make the best of a bad situation.

## CANADIAN LAND

The idea of homestead land in Canada often is discussed by prospective homesteaders, who imagine an immense and beautiful country with few inhabitants and much cheap, fertile land. People have heard especially about the lush meadows, high mountains and sparkling streams of British Columbia, though other provinces are popular, too. While it is certainly true that Canada has a small population for its size and that it can be spectacularly beautiful, it has some drawbacks for homesteaders that we don't always hear about.

First, British Columbia has no crown (public) land that is open to homesteading—at least not in the original sense of claiming land and "proving" your claim. You must buy your land, and at prices of $1000 an acre and higher.

Second, most of the good land already has been taken in B.C. and Ontario—two of the most popular homesteading provinces—and in B.C. only 1½ percent of the land is even considered arable. What land you are likely to find for sale may well be marginal—too poor for the homestead and garden that you would want. Such land may be all right for pasture, but only at a high ratio of acres per cow.

Third, Canada is becoming more and more sensitive about immigrating Americans, as you probably know. You must apply for Landed Immigrant Status, and it may not be granted unless you have a job offer, perhaps a couple of thousand dollars in the bank, proper documents, good health and a good citizenship record.

The following advice to American homesteaders comes from a man who has lived in B.C. for many years:

> You may not even want a farm, but a few acres with house and a couple of horses and work a few days a week or a month in town. Have a garden, a goat, chickens. Great.
>
> But know what you are doing. Too often I have seen Americans come up here, with all their savings, full of learning out of books, soft hands and flabby muscles, and heads jammed with sweet dreams, and go bust—fast!
>
> Come up and welcome. Don't buy your first season. Settle into a nice town or village. There are always houses to rent. Get a part-time job. Drive around. Get to know every old farm and old-timer's cabin. Check prices. Compare prices. Do lots of figuring. Look, look, look, and think, think, think. Then jump in or go home. But don't jump in first and go home busted.

If you are interested in Canada, look into it carefully and sensibly just as you would anywhere. And, as always, take your time and know your skills. Then you'll probably be all right.

People interested in Canadian land should write to the *Dignam Company* (see chapter appendix) for their free brochure and province catalog. Dignam's buys land forfeited for back taxes and re-sells at a profit when the title is clear. Though it is more expensive to buy back-tax land from them, doing so frees you from possible legal tangles over the title. One thing to remember, though, is that land sold for back taxes has a story behind it. The original owner went broke for a reason—perhaps the land is not fit for any kind of farming. Finally: *never, never buy land anywhere without going to see it,* no matter how nice they make it sound.

## FINANCING A LAND PURCHASE

The biggest problem for young homesteaders today in buying land is to find the cash for a down payment or to find the right lender. Certainly the best situation is to pay for it in cash at the time of purchase. But if you cannot afford to do so, here are a few suggestions.

*Conventional mortgage.* Most banks, except in tight money times, arrange mortgages that will cover up to eighty percent of the purchase price. However, you will have to pay the 20 percent down. Also, banks often will not give a mortgage on undeveloped property without habitable buildings. Expect high mortgage rates today and a scarcity of mortgage money even for "good risks," as you may be.

*Second mortgages.* If you don't have enough cash to complete your purchase with a conventional mortgage, a second mortgage sometimes can be arranged with the seller, who will do so to avoid losing a sale. A second mortgage would be for a shorter term than the first.

*Land contract.* If you cannot afford a normal down payment or otherwise swing a bank mortgage you may arrange to buy the land on installments from the seller, who retains title until the contract is paid in full. Be wary of a contract that cancels out credit for payments made, in case of default. You could lose your entire equity if you failed on the 79th payment.

*Savings and loan associations.* S & L companies are a major source of mortagage funds for residential purchases. Terms vary from place to place, and there often is a $40,000 limit on the mortgage.

*Agricultural loans.* Information on agricultural loans is available from the U.S. Department of Agriculture. The following booklets, available from U.S. Government Printing Office, give details of each type of loan:

| Recreation Loans | PA723 | Opportunity Loans | PA663 |
| Conservation Loans | PA799 | Rural Housing Loans | PA476 |
| Co-op Loans | PA662 | Soil & Water Loans | PA972 |
| Operating Loans | PA182 | Watershed Loans | PA406 |
| Forestry Loans | PA624 | Emergency Loans | PA490 |

*Farmers Home Administration* (FHDA). Farmers Home-guaranteed mortgage loans are made for up to 33 years at an interest rate currently of 7½ percent for families with modern income—maximum adjusted income (after taxes) is not more than $10,200. For addresses of local FHDA offices see chapter appendix. Veterans should not overlook G.I. Loan plans available through the Veterans Administration's state offices.

Persons buying in rural areas, it should be noted, need not be "farmers" to qualify for FHDA help.

*Other sources.* Other sources might include private loans from family or friends or a private arrangement with the owner. On one homestead I know of the parents put up the cash. The children are doing the work, and they all live together fairly happily. Best of all, as mentioned, is to use cash savings to buy land outright and start building, using credit there if necessary.

## HOW MUCH CASH IS NEEDED?

It is hard to say just how much cash you need to start homesteading since there are so many variations in land costs and in lifestyles. It's certain, though, that homesteaders today will need much more cash than young people did ten years ago.

Let's assume that you plan to buy ten acres of land at $1,000 an acre. You may need $2,000 for the down payment under commercial financing but perhaps half as much under FHDA. If the land has a habitable building, you may not need to make major renovations immediately, but ten acres with a house is more likely to cost $20-25,000 than $10,000. If it does, your down payment will be closer to $4,000. Add to the down payment, the closing costs (about $300), repair or building costs, purchase of home equipment and general living expenses for the time you estimate will pass until you have a dependable income. A hypothetical breakdown might look like this:

| | | |
|---|---|---|
| Land and house down payment | | $4,000 |
| immediate improvements | | 1,500 |
| one-year period | vehicle | 500 |
| | food | 800 |
| | other-expenses | 1,500 |
| | total | $8,300 |

Granted, for many people it does sound like a lot to have $8,300 in cash at the start of a shoestring venture, and there are undoubtedly circumstances that could reduce this figure considerably. However, a $4,000 down payment on a $25,000 purchase is not high, and total first year living expenses are listed as only $2,800, when they might easily be much higher than that. These figures assume the use of an existing vehicle and no major repair bills over the first year.

If you have a steady income, if you buy less land, if you can build your own house for $2,000, then all these figures might be reduced a little. However, keep in mind that the down payment is only the beginning of your cash needs during the first year; the lower it is, the more likely your other expenses are to equal or surpass it. Probably $5,000 in cash is a bare minimum for anyone thinking about homesteading.

A hard fact, too, is that if you are carrying a big mortgage the annual payment of principal and interest (at current high rates) will be considerable each year—perhaps $2,000 every year for twenty years. Be sure your *cash* income after you start homesteading can sustain this along with other expenses.

## CLOSING THE PURCHASE

### OFFER TO BUY

When you have found a piece of land in the right area and you are satisfied with its price and quality, the first step is to sign an *offer to buy* the property. At the same time you pay a *deposit* toward the purchase as evidence of your good faith. The amount of the deposit varies, but usually will be less than $2,000 on a transaction under $20,000. This deposit is refundable only if you change your mind *before* the seller accepts your offer in writing; after that, you cannot change your mind without losing your deposit—unless you can show gross misrepresentation on the part of the seller. The deposit, of course, is credited toward the down payment that you make when you sign the purchase contract.

### THE PURCHASE CONTRACT

The *purchase* or *sales contract* is drawn up after the seller accepts your initial offer. This contract specifies all the conditions of the sale: fixtures, date of possession, pending insurance, prorating of taxes, an exact description of the property, how the price is to be paid, pre-sale improvements, abstract of title, place of payment and date of deed delivery. Any questions or special conditions, no matter how minor, should be clearly spelled out in the purchase contract to avoid future controversy. The drafting of the purchase contract always should be done by a competent attorney.

### THE DEED

There are two kinds of deeds—*quitclaim* and *warranty* deeds. Do not settle for a quitclaim; it only specifies that the owner relinquishes his claim on the property; it does not guarantee a clear title. A warranty deed requires the seller to defend your claim to the property in the case of some future dispute. Of course, even a warranty deed is not absolute protection; if he were bankrupt at the time, the seller would be in no position to defend your title against other claims.

Even if you have a "clear and perfect title," as well as a carefully drafted purchase agreement, your rights in the land still are subject to legal restrictions. These restrictions may be zoning laws, building codes, covenant restrictions (among adjoining property owners) or environmental regulations. You should know *all* about these first.

### CLOSING AND FILING

The final step in your purchase is the closing, which usually is attended by several people and is held in the office of the seller's lawyer. The seller

and his lawyer will be there, as will you and your lawyer. At the closing any final transactions are accomplished, the purchase price paid, and the deed signed and delivered.

Following the deed delivery, you must file final papers in the town clerk's office or equivalent recording place. Only then is your legal ownership recognized.

## GROUP PURCHASES

Homesteaders today are not quite such "go-it-aloners" as they were a hundred years ago, and those who are more gregarious may start differently. Another way to buy land, now that people are getting used to communes (and communes are getting wiser about themselves), is a *group purchase*. Simply join with two, three or more families to buy a large piece of land, thereby reducing greatly the price per acre. If personal relationships and a basis for sharing the land can be worked out, this arrangement promises reduced costs, increased common land, a built-in social life and an available work force when necessary.

Naturally there are risks in a group purchase—the equitable division of the land and resources being the obvious problem. However, the division often can be agreed upon beforehand and, if necessary, a contract can be drawn up.

If you have friends with nearly the same goals as yours looking for land, you may find a joint purchase of 50 or 100 acres is beneficial. Several small homesteads could be carved from such a parcel. But in some states there are legal limitations or tax penalties on such subdividing. A final caution is simply to know the others well, to be sure that you can be neighbors and still be friends.

## HOMESTEAD DEVELOPMENTS

With steadily rising land values, speculation in land is widespread everywhere. Most land speculators are strictly suburban subdevelopers, but some actually are aiming at the homestead market, advertising one- or two-acre "ranchettes." One development in New Mexico offers half-acre parcels, of which a buyer can buy several adjoining. However, the land primarily is desert, is very flat and dry, and the development is laid out much like any suburban street—not a situation to suit the average homesteader.

Some efforts are being made, however, to assemble land in large tracts and sell off parcels to form homesteaders' intentional communities. One example is *Open Gate,* a group of young homestead-oriented developers in Oregon. They offer four-acre plots, common land and common workshops and a careful community design—certainly a step above most rural developments. At the same time, however, they appear to make little provision in their plans for waste disposal and other design problems inherent in such multi-homestead groupings.

A more diversified communal homestead organization is The Free State of the Ark (headquarters at Box 1198, Stowe, Vermont 05672) which has extensive land holdings in northern New England and Canada. Among the organization's far-ranging activities is a New Pioneer Homestead Program to assist "committed and dedicated people" to get started in homesteading, and when they are unable to obtain down payment and mortgage money the Ark will provide land, some materials and skilled help for building. The new homesteaders are given eleven years to "prove up" their land, agreeing to tithe part of their crops or other products in payment for the land and other assistance received.

No doubt there will be other kinds of homestead developments created in the next few years. While they often provide an easier way for an inexperienced homesteader to get land, they may not be entirely satisfactory, since they greatly reduce the independence of the individual, yet contain all the problems of any organizational endeavor.


## THE EFFECT OF LAND CAPABILITY LAWS

Because of the land speculation boom many rural states are now putting comprehensive land development plans and regulations into effect. Vermont's Act 250, for instance, restricts the number and size of small parcels that a single owner may sell. That state has also enacted a stiff capital gains tax on the sale of land held only a short time, and a law that limits where one can build.

While these laws do not necessarily affect the prospective homesteader, they make it especially important to investigate all relevant legal restrictions before buying land. The help of a lawyer usually is necessary, and with increasing land sale regulations, legal attention will become even more important.

## SUMMARY

If you can do so, live in an area before you buy. Rent a place or stay with friends. Next best is to make frequent visits to the area over several months. As much as possible, know what you are getting into.

Be slow and methodical about making a purchase. As a popular book advises, don't buy land as a surprise for your wife or husband. If you develop a clear idea of what you want, and go about finding it step by step, you still can make a good purchase. And once you have your land, you finally can begin to plan the layout and construction of your homestead.

## APPENDIX

### SUGGESTED READING

LAND ACQUISITION (BOOKS)

Boudreau, Eugene
> Buying Country Land. New York, Collier Books, 1973. 105 pp. $1.95 paperback.

Cobb, Betsy and Hubbard
> City People's Guide to Country Living. New York, Macmillan, 1973. 186 pp. $1.50 paperback.

Moral, Herb
> Buying Country Property. Charlotte, VT, Garden Way Publishing, 1972. 119 pp. $3.00 paperback.

Schwartz, Robert
    Homeowner's Legal Guide. New York, Macmillan, 1969. $1.50 paper-
        back.
Wallin, Craig
    Locating and Buying Low Cost Land. Tucson, Arizona, Box 1949, Wallin
        Publications, 1973. 42 pp. $1.00.
Wren, Jack
    The House Buyer's Guide. New York, Barnes & Noble, 1970. 259 pp.
        $2.50 paperback.
Young, Jean and Jim
    People's Guide to Country Real Estate. New York, Praeger, 1973. $3.95
        paperback.

## PERIODICALS

Campfire Chronicle, Campfire Land Co., Box 254, Appleton, WI 54911
Commerce Business Daily, General Services Admin., 18th & F Streets, N.W.,
    Washington, DC 20405
Your Land (quarterly—$4), Dugent Publishing Corp., 236 E. 46th St., New
    York, NY 10017

## PAMPHLETS

Acquisition of Crown Lands, Land Series Bull. #11, Government Printing
    Bureau, Victoria, B.C.
A Claim on Federal Land, U.S. Bureau of Reclamation, Department of Interior,
    Washington, DC 20240
How To Buy Land, CPC, Box 426, Louisa, Virginia 23093

## LAND MANAGEMENT (BOOKS)

Baker, Jerry
    Make Friends with Your Evergreens and Ground Covers. New York,
        Simon & Schuster, 1973. 95 pp. $1.95 paperback.
Fields, Curtis P.
    The Forgotten Art of Building a Stone Wall. Dublin, NH, Yankee,
        1971. 61 pp. $2.50 paperback.
Garner, Robert J.
    The Grafter's Handbook. New York, Oxford University Press, 1958.
        263 pp. $7.50 hardback.

Guise, Cedric C.
> Management of Farm Woodlands. New York, McGraw-Hill, 1950. $11.30 hardback.

Huxley, Anthony
> Deciduous Garden Trees and Shrubs. New York, Macmillan, 1972. 210 pp. $4.95 hardback.

Kramer, Jack
> Gardening and Home Landscaping. New York, Harper & Row, 1971. $3.50 paperback (Arco).

Smith, J. Russell
> Tree Crops: a Permanent Agriculture. New York, Devin-Adair, 1953. 408 pp. $5.95 hardback.

Sunset Editors
> How to Build Fences and Gates. Menlo Park, CA. Sunset-Lane, 1951. 112 pp. $1.95 paperback.

Taylor, Norman
> The Guide to Garden Shrubs and Trees. Boston, Houghton-Mifflin, 1965. 433 pp. $9.95 hardback.

## DATA SOURCES

Dignam Company, Bloor Street, Toronto, Canada

Division of Land, Department of Nat. Resources, 323 E. 4th Avenue, Anchorage, Alaska 99501

Farmers Home Administration (regional state office listed under U.S. Department of Agriculture in telephone books).

Government Printing Office, Superintendent of Documents, Washington, DC 20402

The Link, Box 48, Danville, Washington 99121 (3 mo. $1)

Open Gate, Route 2, Box 288, McMinnville, OR 97128

Safebuy Real Estate Agency, P.O. Box 589, Little Rock, AR 72203

Strout Realty, 521 E. Green Street, Pasadena, CA 91101 or 1711 North Glenstone, Box 2757, Springfield, MO 65803

United Farm Agency, 612 W. 47th Street, Kansas City, MO 64112

U.S. Bureau of Land Management, Robin Building, 7981 Eastern Avenue, Silver Spring, MD 20910

## TOOLS

If you are buying good quality land without a dwelling already there, you will need a fair amount of equipment with which to construct buildings and to engineer the land to your needs. Included here is a list of tools for landscaping and general land management. It is always wise to pad prices by 10-15% to take into account sales taxes and inflation of prices.

## LAND TOOLS—NON-POWERED

| | |
|---|---:|
| pickaxe | $ 10.00 |
| wood axe | 10.00 |
| sledge hammer | 11.00 |
| shovel | 6.00 |
| bow saw & extra blades | 12.00 |
| rope, 200' of ½ inch manilla | 20.00 |
| grass shears | 5.00 |
| pruning shears | 18.00 |
| wheelbarrow | 40.00 |
| post hole digger | 10.00 |
| fence wire cutter | 5.00 |
| mason's trowel | 4.00 |
| wire stretcher | 20.00 |

## LAND TOOLS—POWERED

| | |
|---|---:|
| chain saw | $100–300.00 |
| cement mixer | 200.00 |

# CHAPTER THREE

# PLANNING AND BUILDING THE HOMESTEAD

Now you have your land, and whether it is small or large, whether it was a bargain or not, you now come to considering the physical layout and building of your homestead. To build what you need you will want to take into account all the existing conditions of the land, the area, the community and your own needs and preferences.

## MAKE A PLAN

As I emphasized in Chapter One, perhaps the most useful things you can do in starting your homestead is to prepare a plan of what you want —not only what activities you will engage in (or what sort of land you need), but what the *physical layout* of your homestead will be. Of course, such a plan can be fully detailed only after you have actually acquired the land. You then must consider all the features of your land and find a suitable relationship to your intended buildings and improvements.

PHYSICAL CONSIDERATIONS

1. *Terrain* will be your first and most obvious consideration. There may be only one possible house site, for instance, or only one that fits in well with other features. Swamps, rocks, trees and exposure all will shape your ideas for building sites.

2. *Water* will affect your homestead layout greatly, depending on its location and quality. You may not have to put in a well or install a pump, if conditions are right.

3. *Existing structures* are important, particularly if they are usable. Even if they are not, they may serve as useful guides to a good or poor house site.

4. *Drainage is essential* for a dry basement, a successful waste disposal system and your gardening. A percolation test should provide the needed information about your soil drainage.

5. The *shape of the lot* will have some influence on your homestead layout. Your building possibilities may be restricted by odd lot lines or rights-of-way.

6. *Road access* may be another important factor. A long driveway can be a serious problem in winter, a steep hill treacherous. Keep in mind also the expense involved in maintaining a private road.

7. *Public utilities* undoubtedly will influence determination of your house site if electricity must be brought in any distance at your expense. You will favor a site as close as possible to existing power lines, that still maintains other house site values.

8. *Climate and weather* will influence the location and positioning of your buildings. Your house should be protected in some way from prevailing winds and winter storms, yet use the sun, too.

9. *Garden areas* would be restricted by poor drainage, slope, or too little sun. If you follow the usual advice of keeping the garden near the house these limitations may affect your house site also.

Many of these land considerations unfortunately are inflexible. The terrain, for instance, is not easily changed to suite your tastes; you must fit your ideas to the lay of the land. Likewise, the location of spring water or utility lines is permanently fixed. So is the shape of your land, at least for now.

Other land factors, such as climate adaptation, weather exposure, garden sites, and even roadways are more flexible. They are areas in which some changes may be worked out. The location of your house and other buildings will depend on developing a suitable relationship among these factors.

All the physical features of your land are thoroughly inter-related, so you must take them all into account more or less at the same time. This can be difficult and frustrating unless you establish your own *order of importance* among them. This order will depend on the basic *goal* of your homestead layout: for efficiency, for low-cost building, for landscape values or whatever. Fortunately a carefully planned, efficient homestead also is usually the most satisfying and attractive.

### VISUALIZING THE HOMESTEAD

To start your homestead layout, draw up a sketch map of your land and locate on it the fixed features, sun orientation and prevailing winds. (If you have a survey map to work from, so much the better.) Such a sketch might look like this:

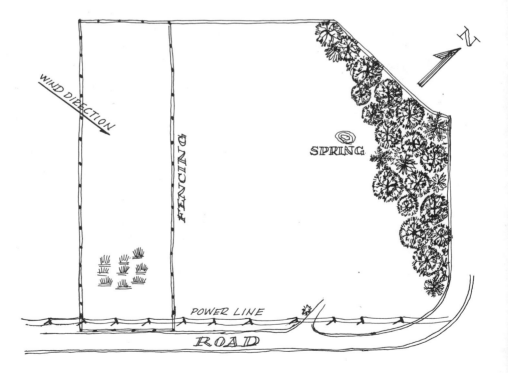

This hypothetical plot of land is partly wooded, has a marshy area in the south corner and comprises five acres. An old fence runs across the land, and utility poles run along the road frontage. A dirt track leads into the field, but shortly ends. Near the woods is a spring that will supply good water all year. (This is obviously an ideal situation that would be rare to find on a small parcel.)

At this point, take up your list of plans for homestead activities and production. It might look like this:

| | |
|---|---|
| vegetable garden (½ acre) | cows (1) 2 quarters living, sleeping |
| fruit trees (4) | house and attached buildings |
| bees | outbuildings |
| hens (6) Chickens | carpentry shop |
| goats (2) | woodshed |

The idea, of course, is to add these items to the map in a trial sketch of your homestead, considering the relationships among the fixed features and among the best production areas. Before actually doing so, however, let's look at a similar hypothetical layout published in 1947 in Ed Robinson's *"Have-More" Plan*. This sequence illustrates the application of an organization idea to the actual homestead grounds.

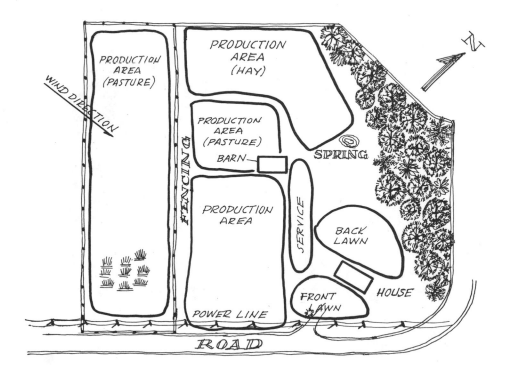

Sketch A shows the homestead use areas in rough form; sketch B shows the refinement of the rough form into buildings and related areas; sketch C shows the detailed expression of these areas in final form. (Note that the plot of land here is very small, probably not more than two acres. Efficient planning still makes a "productive homestead" possible.)

Now let's return to the problem at hand: of incorporating your list of production activities into your own homestead sketch. Undoubtedly the house should be located near the road and utility lines, but set back enough for some privacy. If you think of setting it on the small rise near the trees, keep in mind that added distance up to the house then will be required. Also, the rise probably is a rocky outcropping beneath the humus.

You'll also want the carpentry shop and woodshed to be near or attached to the house. The poultry house and animal barn, however, could be set back, perhaps near the junction of the two pastures. The fruit trees and garden could be placed toward the front of the property, much as they are in the *Have-More* layout. Following the Have-More sequence, here is one suggested solution for this layout problem.

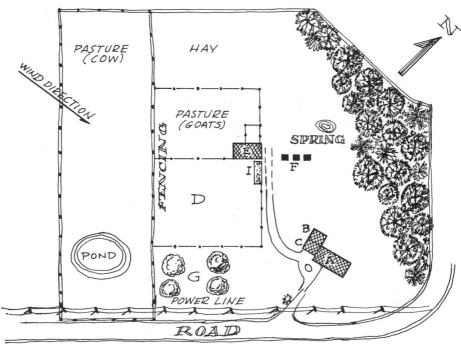

A. HOUSE

B. CARPENTRY SHOP & WOODSHED

C. GARAGE

D. VEGETABLE GARDEN

E. ANIMAL BARN & POULTRY

F. BEEHIVES

G. FRUIT TREES

I. COMPOST

The house is in a good position here, protected as it is by the woods on the north and open to southern sunlight in winter. The driveway not only has been extended to the service area and barn, but has been improved with a turnaround at the road. The woodshed is near the woods, as is the private backyard terrace area. The barn, garden and hayfield are easily accessible by truck.

Naturally there are some disadvantages, in this case the tendency of prevailing winds to bring barn smells toward the house. However, the homestead is organized so that storage and service areas are near the appropriate production areas. Costs of bringing in electric power are kept to a minimum, and pipelines to the spring are almost as short as possible and will feed by gravity to both house and barn. All buildings are protected by the terrain from the severe northerly winds of winter and are situated to make maximum use of the open land.

While this plan perhaps is a good one, many other arrangements might serve just as well. If the barn smell is a problem to you, it might be solved by locating the house approximately where the garden is, giving up the corresponding advantage of easy protection against a northern exposure.

This kind of decision is mostly a matter of individual preference rather than cost, but there are guidelines that are useful in setting up an efficient homestead. Some of them, such as the proximity to power lines, have just been illustrated. Others are more complicated, but they share the common goal of keeping homestead expense and extra work to a minimum.

GUIDELINES FOR HOMESTEAD LAYOUT

Some of the principles that follow are taken from Ed Robinson, "Setting Up a Homestead," part of the *"Have-More" Plan.* Despite their age, they are just as useful today as they were 25 years ago.

1. Use every bit of land advantageously.
2. Keep garden rows a good length for easy cultivation. Run rows north and south for equal sunlight.
3. Fence your pasture into plots for easy rotation. Make pasture gates wide enough for haying and plowing equipment.
4. Plant your vegetable garden near the kitchen for easy access.
5. Locate the compost pile between the barn and garden.

6. Select ground cover and shrubbery that is attractive yet easily cared for. [Alfalfa might substitute for lawn, for example.]
7. Space new trees so that they will not be crowded at maturity.
8. Locate the barn to the lee of the house [which in our place it isn't], but close enough for easy supervision of livestock.
9. Construct proper housing for garden tools, farm equipment, shop tools and other implements. Keep tools in a regular place, preferably as close as possible to the area where they will be used. [Gardenside toolshed, for instance.]
10. Locate house and barn below your spring and as close to it as practical. Consider also the distance to electric power, the length of driveway and the prevailing weather.
11. Provide adequate workshop space for different sorts of work. Install duplicate sets of tools where necessary [barn and garage, for instance].
12. If you heat with wood, build your woodshed handy to house and woodlot.
13. Build a circular driveway to allow easy plowing, if in snow country. Be sure the service area driveway is large enough for truck turning and unloading bulky equipment.
14. Fence your pasture so that animals may be turned loose from the barn. Let fences do double duty wherever possible.
15. Have only as many animals, fruit trees and acres of land as you need. Do not support farm animals as pets; do not allow land or produce to go unused.

## BUILDING HOMESTEAD STRUCTURES

When you begin a rough layout it is not necessary to know exactly what buildings you will need besides the house and related workshops. However, as your homestead plan becomes more detailed you must decide what kind of homestead activities you will have and what buildings these will require. The most common, of course, are a chicken house, a small barn for a few goats or cow, and a woodshed.

In meeting these building needs you will have to take several factors in account: existing buildings (if any), the cost of the building materials, community zoning, building codes, building functions, design preferences and your own skills.

## EXISTING BUILDINGS

If there are existing structures on your land you may be able to make considerable use of them. If the house is not habitable, too far gone or completely unsuitable, it still may be useful as a temporary shelter, either for you or for your animals. Or it may be a source of lumber for other structures. If it *is* habitable your building needs are reduced dramatically, at least for the time being.

BUILDING MATERIALS

Your choice of building materials will depend on three things: the cost, the availability and your own experience in working with these materials. Generally it is best to use *indigenous materials,* since they are cheaper (or free) and reflect the character of the land. The Nearings, for instance, chose to build stone houses, partly because of the remarkable abundance of stone on their land. In a forest a log house might be the most obvious and appropriate building. Availability and cost generally are related, and you probably will find the selection of materials that are both cheap and accessible is narrow.

What may determine your choice, if you plan to do the building yourself, is your own skill. An experienced carpenter would be wasting his talents to set out for the first time on a building of stone. However, if all your skills are limited you might as well choose the sort of material and building that seems to be the most useful—that is, that you expect to be dealing with again and again. Your basic choice is among logs, timbers and boards, and stone. More unusual materials would be canvas, foam or prefabricated metal structures, as we will see later.

COMMUNITY ZONING

The structures you build, as well as the enterprises you start, may depend to some degree on zoning laws. Many rural areas have no zoning laws at all, but many states, such as Oregon, have begun zoning plans for the entire state. If you are thinking of a residential homestead only, you will probably be all right. But if you plan to build a sawmill or a furniture factory, an early check with the county or town zoning board is essential.

If you live in a semi-suburban area you may have problems with farm animal restrictions. Whatever your doubts or questions about the local zoning, check with local officials, though of course you should have done so when choosing your land.

BUILDING CODES

Although some rural areas have no building codes, many others do. These codes often regulate the way your house must be constructed, and occasionally they specify that a licensed electrician or plumber must do the work. Most often they relate to water and sewage systems. Before getting too far involved in building plans find out exactly how local building codes will affect you.

Occasionally you can circumvent building codes, as do the people who simply label their unusual dwellings as "storage sheds" or "tent platforms." Generally, though, this is dangerous, particularly if the local building code is being used as a harassment against unwanted newcomers. This sort of thing can run you into trouble with local officials, who can force you to tear down the structure in question or rebuild to conform to the code.

In spite of the political ramifications of the building codes, they are basically designed to keep you from erecting an unsafe dwelling—obviously a beneficial precaution. So take the trouble to find out about the codes and abide by them.

### FUNCTION AND DESIGN

If *what* you build depends on your need, and what materials you *use* to build it depends on the locale, its *design* is a combination of these and your personal taste. Very few people would take the time and trouble to build a woodshed from stone—but Scott Nearing did just that. He liked stone.

Designing a functional and sound building is not easy for the amateur, though it can be immensely satisfying if it works out. A house in particular is your chance to show the world just what kind of place you think a man should live in. But in reaching a final design for your house or other structures you will want to keep constantly in mind that a building is most satisfying when it *serves* your needs rather than frustrates them.

## HOUSES FOR HOMESTEADING

The considerations involved in building a homestead or adapting an existing house are discouragingly many. But you can start by grouping them under a few categories: house costs and economics, house siting on the land (much of which we have already discussed), and the physical layout of a country house.

ECONOMICS

As mentioned earlier, there has been a tremendous rise the past ten years in the cost, not only of land, but also of house construction. A few years back it was perfectly possible to buy ten acres and a small house for $5-6,000. Mortgage payments might have been $60 a month— something a small family could manage.

Today the rising markets in rural areas have quadrupled the prices, sometimes to $50,000 or more, of something that would have cost you $15,000 not long ago. A lovely white farmhouse with a couple of red barns is simply beyond the reach of most young people who want to move to the country. In many areas old houses in good condition cannot be found at anything like a reasonable price.

One alternative is to locate an old farm that is honestly run-down— perhaps an unpainted old farmhouse that exposes cracks to the winter wind, and a sagging old barn. Unfortunately, old country places in really terrible shape often require renovation that costs as much as or more than building a new house. Lumber has risen 90 percent or more in the last year, and many other standard building materials have followed suit. Of course old houses can be restored, but sometimes only at many times the original cost. The only benefit here is that you sometimes can spread this cost over several years by making improvements as you have money available.

The situation comes down to this: any place you buy with an old house on it that has much useful land at all, very probably is going to cost you more than $20,000. If the house is in good shape it may cost much, much more. With as few as ten acres, you may be talking about $35,000 and up. Immediately you are involved in a long-term mortgage with heavy payments. And then you are only a little better off than the suburban homeowner. Of course, it is sometimes possible to find just the right place at a bargain, but these occasions are so rare (and getting rarer) that it hardly seems worthwhile to hope in that direction.

Buying a house or a house and land is much the same in one respect as buying only land. It's a mistake to buy (or pay for) more of a house than you can afford, tying up your limited capital unnecessarily. (You will have plenty of other uses for your savings later on.) However, one way out is to follow the example of the original homesteaders by building your own house.

Building a house is not impossibly difficult for most people. Remember, too, that the pioneers managed to do it with less useful tools than you have. Admittedly, there are many things to learn and many mistakes to avoid, but it is being done all the time. In *Walden,* Thoreau asked, "Shall we always resign the pleasure of construction to the carpenter?" Particularly for homesteaders, the answer can be *no.* Not only is it fun to build your own house, but you can probably do it (to get back to the point) for about half the cost of a comparable buy, especially if you make a determined effort to cut cash expenses.

## HOUSE SITING

The immediate problem in building a new house on a homestead is its precise location. The site must meet the necessary needs for water drainage, soil porosity, road access, weather protection and good homestead organization, some of which already have been mentioned.

*Water,* of course, is the first consideration. If your land has a spring, your house should be located downhill, as I have illustrated. Sometimes this is not possible or desirable, but even then the location of your water source is a primary concern.

*Drainage* is equally important. Surface water must be able to drain away from your house, not into the basement. Your septic system must be able to discharge into the soil, as well as be installed right in the first place. The best location, therefore, is a slight slope, free of tree roots and subsurface boulders.

*Soil porosity* will be important for the operation of the septic system and for any excavation (which will be necessary even if you do not have a conventional basement). Digging a hole is the best test for soil makeup and the distance to bedrock.

As I said before, *road access* obviously is necessary, and the easier the better. Be wary of building your house with a steep driveway; you may be constantly plagued with washouts and stuck vehicles. If your soil is mostly clay, be prepared to add ditches and lots of gravel to make the roadway passable in wet weather.

*Weather* and *climate* are factors that too many people more or less

overlook—to their own disadvantage. Houses in a northern climate should be protected on the north and west from winter storms. Outbuildings, a hill, or a windbreak of trees all can be useful. Similarly northern houses should face south, so the windows can take advantage of the winter sun.

It is also wise to situate your house so that the prevailing winds blow from the house to the barn, unlike our earlier homestead sketch. Find out how drifting snow might plug your intended driveway.

Finally, keep in mind the homestead organization—that is, the relation of your house to garden, barn and workshops. Notice in the several layout sketches that the house, garage and workshop areas actually are attached, and that these in turn are easily accessible to the barn, service area, hayfield and woodlot. Deciding on the best location for these production buildings may indicate an obvious house site, while choosing a house site first may create later conflicts with your production needs.

Generally the house location is not a problem. It is simply an exercise in common sense. Look at the older farmhouses in your area for ideas (though you need not place your barn to block the best view as they used to do). Houses that have stood the test of time usually are well suited to the earth, sun and weather.

### BUILDING FOR COUNTRY LIVING

Once you have bought your land, prepared your homestead layout and decided on a final house site, you are ready to plan exactly what kind of house you want—not only the construction style, but the internal layout as well. Unlike a suburban home, a homestead house is an essential part of overall homestead production, so its design is worth very careful thought.

The major difference between the conventional house and productive homestead is the vastly greater number of activities that occur in a country home. In your planning, therefore, consider all the homestead activities it may encompass. Such a list might look like this:

    meal preparation & serving
    bathroom
    sleeping
    laundry
    entertainment
    vegetable canning
    freezing
    milk separation, and butter and cheese making
    washing utensils and equipment
    food storage
    fuel storage
    meat cutting & handling
    herb drying
    honey extraction
    sewing/weaving
    office work

Your list may not include all of these items, especially at first, but eventually it may be at least this long.

Most of these activities, such as meals, milk separation, and vegetable canning will be done in the kitchen. Because of this, a large harvest kitchen in a country house is more than a pleasant tradition—it is a necessity. If you start with an existing house that has a small kitchen, you might build a separate harvest room for canning, freezing produce, cheese making and for many other related chores, keeping your original kitchen for daily meal preparation. The particular usefulness of the harvest kitchen and its precise differences from most modern kitchens have been explained in Ed Robinson's "Layout for a Harvest Kitchen" (see chapter appendix).

SPECIAL AREAS: HOUSE-RELATED FUNCTIONS

Many aspects of production that ordinarily would be handled in the house sometimes can be relegated effectively to their own rooms or areas. Rather than using the harvest room, for instance, you might find a separate *milk, cheese and butter room* useful.

Similarly, though, an area in the harvest room could be set aside for canning garden vegetables at harvest time. For canned goods, vegetable and fruit storage, portions of the basement could be fitted with shelves and properly kept dry and cool. A basement area also may be useful if the temperature is right for making vinegars, cider, wine, beer, sauerkraut and other pickled products.

Few families require a large walk-in *freezing room,* but many home-steaders have large freezers located in the basement or garage. Freezers are standard items for the storage of hundreds of pounds of meat, vegetables and fruit.

While the harvest kitchen may suffice, a *honey room,* if you get into bees, is useful for the extraction of honey and packing in jars and cans. Because it is a messy process, an easily washable floor and counter are essential. Also possibly needed, and perhaps in the harvest room, is a special area for incubating eggs or a cold box for egg storage.

If you plan to raise beef cattle or hogs, perhaps a *butchering shed* should be built (or improvised if your butchering is done only once or twice a year). This might be combined with a meat handling area, or this perhaps with a *smoke house,* which can be as small as three feet square and only six feet high.

In the country, where a lot of clothes get dirty often, a *laundry room* really is a necessity. Its best location is near the kitchen and an outside entrance, so that dirty work clothes can be disposed of directly. This also is a good place for a *mud room* for hanging children's wet and dirty clothes and for muddy boots. A very welcome item here is a small washroom which allows the family to clean up *before* making the in-evitable trek across the kitchen floor.

Finally, every country house should have lots of closet, shelf and storage space, wide hallways, and easy access between related areas. If you plan a *sewing* or *weaving room,* on the second floor for example, be

sure that doorways and stairs are wide enough for moving looms as well as normal furniture.

BASEMENTS

Basements today are somewhat controversial—some argue against them and others swear by them. Most old houses *do* have basements, and they were useful for storage, as root cellars, and as locations for old-fashioned gravity heating systems. If you can afford the excavation cost, a basement today can still be useful for the same reasons, especially if it has outside, bulkhead access.

The disadvantages of basements are their cost and their tendency to be damp, sometimes causing rotting of supporting timbers. The availability of alternative heating systems makes a basement a matter of personal choice. You pay more but you get additional space and a built-in root cellar; you pay less (perhaps) and build on a slab. For those who are undecided, there are many books that discuss the pros and cons of basement construction. (See also the discussion of pole construction for a related alternative.)

There are many good books available on the design and building of country houses. Particularly worth your while are *Your Engineered House* by Rex Roberts, *Layout for a Productive Homestead* by Ed Robinson, and *The Owner-Built Home and Homestead* by Ken Kern. (See chapter appendix.)

## TYPES OF HOUSES

WOOD FRAME HOUSES

Most houses you see are of wood frame construction. They have many advantages, among them the huge common fund of construction knowledge, and the geometry involved in right angles and straight surfaces. They are easier to learn about, easier to build (in some ways), and easier to fit things into. Another advantage of the conventional frame is the *availability of financing*. Banks are much more interested in financing a standard type of house—something they can readily sell (if they are forced to foreclose)—than an "oddball" house built for eccentric tastes. Financing alone is one reason why millions of people live in basic suburban houses that look so much alike. "Ranch style" or "split level" houses don't have much personality, but usually they are easier to buy and sell.

The *disadvantage* to conventional houses is cost. A small suburban house built by a contractor with union labor simply has to cost $20,000 minimum, because of the prices of lumber and labor time involved. Because of these costs, we are in something of a housing crisis, with many people forced to live in trailers or substandard housing. But others are experimenting with unusual materials and building their own houses.

Most homesteaders either buy land with an old house on it or build one to suit themselves. Wood frame construction still is the most common, and some ways to cut these costs are listed toward the end of the chapter. However, the last few years houses have been blossoming out in many new styles and materials. One of the great advantages we have over the builders of the past is the immense new technology, particularly in new materials and building concepts. Nothing prevents you from building a nineteenth-century-model frame house, but some other kinds of houses can be built cheaper and quicker.

I won't go into detail about new house styles (which would require a book in itself), but here are a few comments on alternative houses and their general advantages and disadvantages.

POLE BUILDINGS

Pole buildings are not houses built *of* poles, but houses built *on* poles, which are about the size of telephone poles. These houses can be built quite cheaply ($4-5,000), because they do not require conventional foundations; the weight of the house is borne by the poles, which also serve as a frame. Another advantage of pole houses is their adaptability to steep hillsides and other terrain unsuitable for excavation. Installation of poles does not disturb much topsoil or create erosion problems.

Except for the weight limitation on the poles, the disadvantage of pole construction lies mainly in the need for extra insulating of the floor area, which is exposed. Pole houses might cost somewhat more to heat for this reason, and be better suited to warmer climates. For more infor-

mation, see the FHA booklet, *Pole House Construction,* and also *Pole Building Construction,* Garden Way Publishing Co.

## LOG CABINS

The log cabin is one of the oldest kinds of pioneer houses in America. Logs were always free for the cutting in pioneer days and the cost of the house consisted entirely of labor time and feeding the neighbors who came to lend a hand.

Today a log cabin may cost substantially more, but it still can be cheaply built. If you have your own source of connifers, you still can cut your logs and haul them to the site in classic style. Many books explain the techniques of log building, and you can probably find friends or neighbors who know a few tricks and are willing to work on a cabin.

The major cash needs will be insulation, plumbing, windows, roofing materials, flooring and electric wiring; they might come to $5,000 or so, depending on materials and shortcuts used, and size.

## DOMES

During the past few years Buckminster Fuller's geodesic domes have been an "in" kind of house. A dome can be built any size, from a tiny egg to an astrodome, depending on what you want. The same is true of materials to some degree, though using plywood is common (and expensive). Domes have been built in Drop City from the tops of junked autos; they have also been sold in expensive kits by design companies. Generally a dome can be built for what you have to spend—perhaps between $200 and $10,000.

Domes have certain disadvantages—the most noticeable being the absence of flat walls and square corners, which means a lot of space is wasted. Also interior walls must be built to stand independently; they cannot be supported by the dome. For these reasons, many dome dwellers choose to have an open dome interior, setting aside certain areas for work, sleeping and eating.

Another problem is ventilation, since windows must be clear sections of the shell. One group of dome people found that their bright, airy dome soon created an unpleasant "greenhouse" effect, despite the heat vent at the top.

Like many alternative houses, domes are not necessarily the best structure to link with other outbuildings and homestead functions. People do choose them because they're fun, and because they symbolize a break with old ways or establishment values.

## STONE HOUSES (AND BRICK)

Stone houses have had periods of popularity, especially in areas where good building stone was plentiful. Northern states, such as Wisconsin,

Pennsylvania and New York have a good number of stone houses, most of which were built in the nineteenth century.

The advantages of a stone house are partly intangible: a certain beauty and impression of strength. In addition, stone is one of the cheapest building materials, since usually it can be gathered simply for the labor. To some degree building with stone has been popularized by Scott and Helen Nearing in *Living the Good Life,* which may spur new builders to look seriously at their experience.

The main disadvantage with stone is that it is heavy, and building by hand is a ponderous operation. Stone also suggests cold and rigidity, but cold can be cured with insulation, and earthquakes are few except on the west coast.

Saving money on stone construction is dependent on getting the stones at the site and doing the building yourself—not the sort of homefixing project that one accomplishes in a few weeks. (The Nearings spent several years on some of their buildings and probably had one under construction all the time.)

If you seriously want to build with stone you had better have another house to live in meanwhile. In the end, though, a stone house is something that may last hundreds of years and will become almost an outgrowth of the rocky soil around it.

## YURTS

One of the most unusual wood structures to appear in recent years is the *yurt,* a round wooden sort of tipi originally used (with skins) by Mon-

golian nomads. A yurt has no frame as such, but is held together by a cable encircling the wall boards, which support the roof with its circular skylight.

Yurts are not difficult to construct but they do require a good understanding of and adherence to the principles involved. One communal homestead that uses yurts estimates that two persons can construct a yurt in as little as two days, not counting the gathering of materials. The cost may vary from $1 to $600, depending on the material and construction style.

Building plans for yurts can be obtained from Bill Coperthwaite in Bucks Harbor, Maine. His Yurt Foundation is responsible for much of their popularization in this country.

## TIPIS

Several homesteaders have written to me about their experiences living in tipis, though most have lived in one only temporarily. Tipis were used as year-round homes by the Plains Indians, however, and can be used in fair comfort at surprisingly low temperatures. They are best suited to flat open areas like prairies, and become less practical in sloping or wet sites.

The unbeatable advantage of a tipi is its low cost and quick construction time (about a half hour once the poles are ready to go). Tipi kits (minus poles) are available for about $200, or you can make one following a pattern. The best book on tipis, according to everyone I've talked to, is *The Indian Tipi* by Gladys and Reginald Laubin. (Also listed in chapter appendix are tipi manufacturers.)

Unfortunately, tipis are probably not suited to permanent homesteading, if for no other reason than their size. They do not provide the sort of production, living and storage space which we need, but they still are fun and useful as temporary dwellings on a beginning homestead.

## UNDERGROUND HOUSES

*The Mother Earth News* has published a couple of articles about "natural" homes, such as houses dug into the ground. One such house, for instance, was built underground for roughly $50—the cost of the plastic sheeting used to keep it dry. Other costs were eliminated by using lumber mill ends, friends' labor, and rough logs cut by hand. The house has no plumbing, no electricity, and a dirt floor—not elegant, but one alternative for those who wish to live very cheaply.

Without belaboring the obvious, there are some disadvantages to underground homes—mostly drainage and moisture. In the house just mentioned, the plastic sheeting outside and a wood stove inside helped to keep the house dry.

The underground houses have surprising advantages: no insulation problem, no fire danger, no exterior maintenance, and excellent protection against storms, wind, and summer heat. Despite these benefits, most homesteaders probably will prefer to pay more and live on the earth rather than in it.


MODULAR HOUSES AND TRAILERS

We have mentioned that rising land costs have forced many rural people into house trailers in trailer "cities" or on small plots of land. Trailers seemed to many people to offer cheap, ready-made housing that required little or no maintenance. Unfortunately this benefit is largely a myth. Despite the steady demand for trailers, buyers are often finding repair service nonexistent, warranties deceptive, and trailers themselves a poor buy for homestead living.

Similar to trailers in concept are "modular" homes, such as the "flying saucer" *Futuro* home. These dwellings, by contrast, are sold as vacation or second homes to people who already own conventional homes. Modular homes can be installed practically anywhere, and do not require much site preparation. They are built to be single, self-contained units, not unlike a space ship planted in foreign soils.

Trailers and modular homes seem poorly suited to homesteaders, however, except perhaps as temporary housing. They have no real work or storage space, must be constantly maintained, and have a low resale value. Equally important, they also seem out of harmony with the land. To live in a steel and chrome box in the midst of fields and woods seems to show a certain lack of rapport with nature.

### KITS AND READY-BUILT HOMES

For those who wish to avoid trailers, but who do not feel capable of (or interested in) building their own house, one of the ready-built houses may be ideal. A home "kit" usually consists of prefabricated parts; what you do is to put it together.

*Vermont Log Homes,* for instance, sells a pre-cut log cabin that can be assembled by two men. The logs are milled with two flat edges; they fit together with splines. One typical model features a living room/kitchen, bath, sleeping loft, and front porch. It costs somewhat under $9,000, but requires that you provide the foundation and add your own flooring, plumbing, roofing and electricity.

The problem with such kits, in spite of their fairly natural appearance, is that you pay for the materials, for the design, and for the packaging. If you have more money than time to spend, a kit like this may still be a good buy. Most homesteaders, though, will find that their time spent gathering free or cheap materials will allow them to build an equivalent home for even less. (See chapter appendix for additional manufacturers.)


### FOAM HOUSES

A final offbeat idea for alternative houses involves the use of polyurethane foam which can be sprayed on any form to provide excellent insulation. It can also be used to create complete abstract houses, based on a chicken wire form.

The esthetic properties of a "spray-on" house like this seem great: the whole construction could take a couple of days, not counting the setting up of chicken wire. Built-in furniture, sleeping alcoves, interior walls could all be sprayed into existence. Total cost is hard to predict, but insulation foaming of a dome usually costs about $1,000. For a foam *house,* naturally, there would be many extra costs. The work usually must be done by a contractor who has the special equipment needed.

The disadvantages of foam houses would seem to be their questionable durability. While they might be cheaper than conventional houses, they would be relatively costly and artificial as an alternative home. So few people have built this sort of house so far that it is impossible to know its usefulness.

## GENERAL COMMENTS

There are other types of construction that could have been mentioned, both conventional and offbeat. You may well have an unusual house in mind that would be cheap and practical for homesteading. Bear in mind, however, several considerations in choosing an alternative house:

First, a homestead house must be built to last *and* to be comfortable. Exotic experiments with foam or domes may be fun, but eventually they may not prove so satisfactory as a more time-tested house, especially for country living.

Second, things accumulate on a homestead. A well-organized house is essential to maintain an efficient operation. An alternative house usually cannot have the storage space, workshop space, and other facilities that you will find necessary. They can be used, of course (though people in trailers will find themselves at a special disadvantage). But generally speaking, a conventional *country* house, if well designed, will have all of the things you need.

Third, financing for an unconventional house usually is hard to secure.

In thinking of different types of buildings, try to find people who have built the sort of house you want; go visit them and get their advice. Much can be learned by someone else's unsuccessful experiment.

## CUTTING CONSTRUCTION COSTS

Whatever type of house and building material you choose, there are ways to save construction costs that will allow you to have what you want at a fraction of "normal" market prices.

*1* First, *do the building yourself.* Most building methods are fairly standard, and you probably can learn everything you need to know if you're willing to work at it and do a lot of reading. To save the labor costs makes a tremendous difference, and with a little help from your friends you can do just that.

*2* Second, *don't go to an expensive architect* for your house plans. Draw

up as detailed a design as you can and find an architect/builder who will go over it with you to suggest practical changes. There are plenty of carpenters and freelance builders who will work on a personal, friendly project like yours on a consulting basis.

Third, *become a scavenger.* Pick up mill ends at the sawmill. Find out where to pick up rolls of imperfect or slightly damaged roll roofing. Buy windows, doors, other fixtures and timbers second-hand. In short, don't pay top dollar for topnotch materials. Use odds and ends. For instance, old silos make excellent flooring and often are available for the trouble of pulling them down; the same is true of old barns and abandoned houses. We're lucky enough to live in a wasteful society that has lots of very useful things in its junkpiles. Recycle them.

Fourth, *build only what you need or can afford.* The entire homestead or house need not be built overnight. It may take years to complete all the projects you first envisioned—even finishing the house. Sometimes, if you have enough cash for only a couple of rooms, it's practical to go ahead

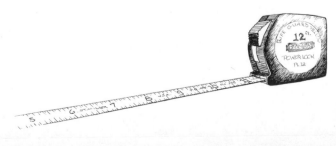

and build them, using them for living quarters until you are able to complete the rest of the home. The important thing is to have a detailed plan and carry it steadily to fulfilment.

Fifth, *avoid cash expenditures.* Wherever possible, arrange to barter or swap services with your friends and neighbors if you need their help. This will not be too difficult, especially if you have some useful skills of your own.

Sixth, *plan ahead.* One way Scott Nearing saved money was to plan a year or more ahead for his building and homestead needs. In this way he could take advantage of the lowest cash prices for the materials he needed, buying cement or lumber and storing it until the building day arrived.

Seventh, *buy in large lots. Take advantage of special deals.* Chances are that you will have recurring needs for cement, fencing, fertilizer and other non-perishable bulk items that may be cheaper in large lots. Save money later by buying more than you need initially and keeping the surplus at hand. Also offer to pick up your materials from the warehouse if that will save a few cents a bag. Make it easy for the supplier to deal with you.

There are many good books on cheap building techniques for the amateur builder. Read them—not just one, but several. Get a good, all-around view of what you're trying to do and what most authorities feel is the best and cheapest way to do it. Every book will have a few tips that you can jot down and use later when you need them. I particularly recommend Rex Roberts, *Your Engineered House* and Herb Moral, *Buying Country Property.*

_stopped here_

## PROTECTING YOUR INVESTMENT

As you probably know, one of the privileges that goes with owning a $40,000 house in the suburbs is paying premiums for fire, theft and accident insurance. As the companies say, with that kind of an investment (or debt), you can't afford not to. If you plan to sell eventually, you also must keep an eye on exterior maintenance.

To get bank financing, however, you as a homesteader will have to take out comprehensive fire insurance. And even if you do not have a mortgage, insurance is a wise idea. So much time and energy may be invested in the contents of your home that you can hardly afford to begin again, even apart from the expense of the building. If you have built a cheaper home, however, you will pay correspondingly less for insurance because you (and the bank) have less to lose.

## OTHER HOMESTEAD STRUCTURES

Besides a home for yourself, you probably will be building housing for your livestock and adequate storage sheds and workshops. Following are a few short sketches of these buildings and their important features.

### WOODSHED

If you heat with wood or only have a fireplace, you will need a shed to store dry firewood, which is best cut one year in advance (as we will dis-

cuss later), and allowed to season. For this reason the shed should be big enough to hold enough wood for an entire winter and allow ventilation. As shown on the earlier sketch it should be logically located near the house and the woodlot.

## POULTRY HOUSE

If you plan to have hens, you will need a henhouse and poultry run. The henhouse need not be large, but should provide protection from cold and rain. A good arrangement (see sketch) is a wire mesh floor that will allow droppings to fall through and be removed readily. Henhouses are the ideal places for using odd pieces of lumber, roofing material and chicken wire.

Plans for poultry houses of varying sizes are available from several sources (see chapter appendix).

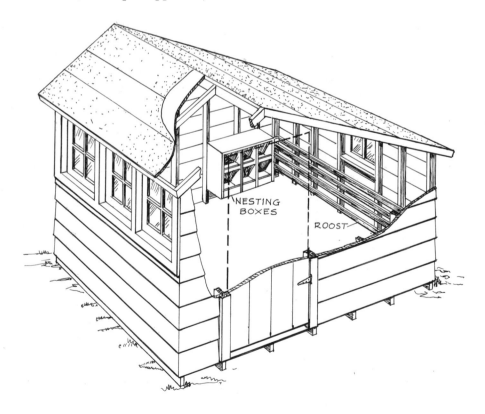

## SMALL BARN

For a few cows or goats, rabbits, pigs or a horse, a small barn will be needed. Often an existing building can be used adapted at moderate cost by partitioning it into the stalls and other necessary areas.

If you need a new barn but want something small, the *"Have-More" Plan* includes an excellent small barn design. You might consider a pole barn also. (See chapter sources.) Erecting a small barn is not a difficult job: what you are doing is just building an elaborate shed with arrangements for stalls, feeding areas, and hay or grain storage.

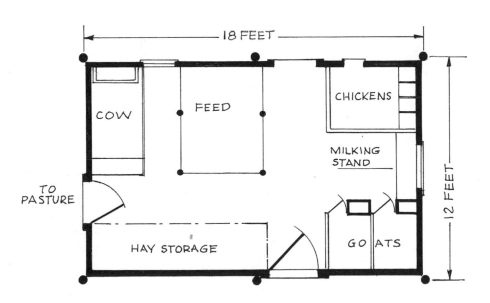

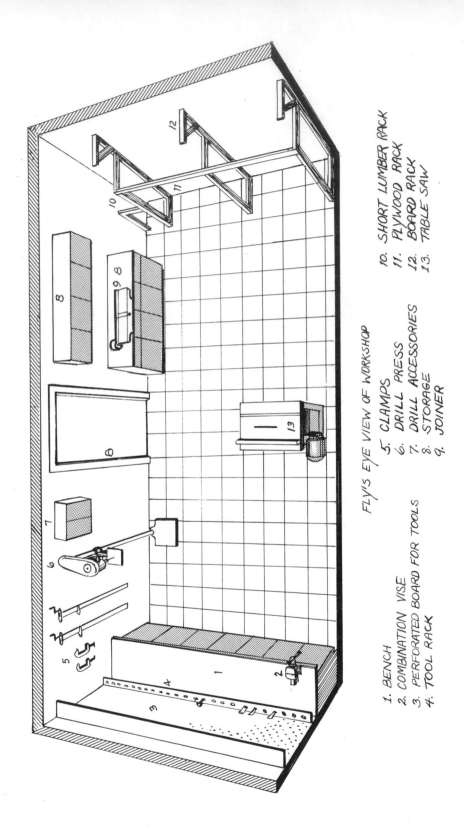

FLY'S EYE VIEW OF WORKSHOP

1. BENCH
2. COMBINATION VISE
3. PERFORATED BOARD FOR TOOLS
4. TOOL RACK

5. CLAMPS
6. DRILL PRESS
7. DRILL ACCESSORIES
8. STORAGE
9. JOINER

10. SHORT LUMBER RACK
11. PLYWOOD RACK
12. BOARD RACK
13. TABLE SAW

It is a good idea, as shown on the earlier layout, to locate your barn so that animals may be turned out to pasture directly. In the case of chickens, a poultry run could be attached to the barn area, an arrangement that will save time and effort.

## WORKSHOP

A workshop is essential on a homestead. It should be light, dry, airy and screened, with a tight floor and some means for heating in winter. Shop doors should be wide enough to admit large and cumbersome equipment and materials, perhaps eight feet wide. Also a good idea are built-in workbenches and a careful arrangement of tools for easy use. Electrical outlets for power equipment are essential. A workshop often is wisely attached to the house or garage, where it is close to power and heat sources and the driveway service area.

## GARDEN HOUSE

A separate garden house is a good idea. It contains benches, bins, cupboards, space for flats, and possibly tool, fence and fertilizer storage. Naturally, it should be located near the garden. Garden tools also might be kept in a separate tool shed or the garage, where moisture cannot affect them.

## GREENHOUSE

Avid gardeners often wish to continue their plant work all year, for which some kind of greenhouse is necessary. If you live in a moderate climate, a separate greenhouse can be constructed with a wood frame and clear plastic sheeting that requires no artificial heat. In a colder northern climate, a small greenhouse could be attached to a heated room that would be easily accessible from the house. Sometimes simply a large three-sided window area is sufficient—a feature easily planned into the original house

construction. You also can plan to do container gardening or start plants under lights elsewhere in the house or other heated area.

### MAPLE-SAP EVAPORATOR HOUSE

If you have sugar maple trees, you may wish to make your own maple syrup or produce it as a cash crop. In either case, a "sugar house" is necessary for the prolonged boiling of maple sap that is required. Such a hut need not be elaborate and should be located at or near the maple orchard. (For more information about this, read the Nearings, *The Maple Sugar Book*.)

## GARAGE/TOOL SHED

For winter vehicle protection a garage is very useful. It also provides a place for necessary mechanical work and storage for machine tools and parts. It gives you a dry, well-lighted place to do tractor or auto repair work on rainy days.

If your carpentry shop is small, the garage may also be useful for storage of general homestead tools. As we shall discuss in a later chapter, tools should be carefully handled, treated and stored for maximum life. Tools and equipment left lying in the weather are soon useless, and without a regular storage location, they tend to have disappeared when you need them most.

### OTHER AREAS

There are many activities that take place on a homestead for which a special building is required. Other possible production areas that might be planned include a paint room, forge, feed room, harness and tack room, potter's shed, shipping corner, sawmill, machine shop, construction supply room, or pump house.

Sometimes a corner for storage, a shelf in the garage is all that is needed. Of course, you may find also that the buildings listed above are not the most important ones, and in that case, you must plan the structure or workshop arrangement that best suits your own needs.

## SUMMARY

The satisfactory homestead is logical, well-planned and efficient. This planning begins with the acquisition of the land and in some ways it never ends. Terrain, housing, fields, driveway and workshops are all related to each other in a sensible fashion. Proper housing is provided for livestock; proper storage and work space is arranged for tools and production activities. The house in particular is organized to accommodate the many aspects of living and homestead work. In this way, long-run expenses are kept to a minimum, and you enjoy the fullest satisfaction of being a homesteader.

# APPENDIX

## SUGGESTED READING AND EQUIPMENT SOURCES FOR HOME CONSTRUCTION AND REMODELING

FRAME HOUSE, CONSTRUCTION & REMODELING

Anderson, L. O.
> Wood Frame House Construction. Agriculture handbook #73. Washington, U.S.D.A., 1970. 223 pp. $2.25 paperback.

Anderson, L. O. & Zornig, Harold F.
> Build Your Own Low-Cost Home. New York, Dover Publications, 1972. 204 pp. $4.95 paperback.

Boericke, Arthur
> Handmade Houses: A Guide to the Woodbutcher's Art. San Francisco, Scrimshaw Press, 1973. $12.95.

Boyd, James S.
> Practical Farm Buildings. Danville, Illinois, The Interstate, 1973. 265 pp. $7.95 paperback.

Canadian Wood-frame House Construction (free)
> Canadian Central Mortgage and Housing Corp.
> 650 Lawrence Avenue West
> Toronto 7, Ontario, Canada

Cobb, Hubbard H.
> How to Buy and Remodel the Older House. New York, Collier, 1970. 519 pp. $3.95 paperback.

Dietz, Albert George Henry
> Dwelling House Construction. Cambridge, MIT Press, 1971. 396 pp. $3.95 paperback.

Kahn, Lloyd
> Shelter. New York, Random House, 1973. $5.00 paperback.

Kern, Ken
> The Owner-built Home. Oakhurst, California, Ken Kern Drafting, 1961. 276 pp. $5.00 paperback.

Roberts, Rex
> Your Engineered House. Philadelphia, J. B. Lippincott, 1964. $8.95 hardback.

Robinson, Ed
>Layout for a Harvest Kitchen. Charlotte, VT, 1974. $2.50.

Low-Cost Wood Homes for Rural America (construction manual)

Wood Frame House Construction, Agriculture Handbook #73
>Superintendent of Documents, U.S. Government Printing Office
>Washington, D.C. 20402

### GENERAL, CONSTRUCTION & REMODELING

Conklin, Groff
>The Weather-Conditioned House. New York, Reinhold Publishing Company, 1958.

Foss, E. W.
>Construction and Maintenance for Farm & Home. New York, John Wiley & Sons, 1960. $10.95 hardback.

Johnston, R. W.
>The Book of Country Crafts. New York, A. S. Barnes & Co., 1973. $3.98

Olgyay, Victor
>Design with Climate. Princeton, N.J., Princeton University Press, 1963. $25.00 hardback.

Schmidt, John L.; Lewis, Walter H.; Olin, Harold Bennett
>Construction: Principles, Materials and Methods. Chicago, American Savings & Loan Institute Press, 1970. $14.95 paperback (Interstate).

Schuler, Stanley
>All Your Home Building and Remodeling Questions Answered. New York, Macmillan, 1971. 534 pp. $8.95 hardback.

Schwartz, Robert & Cobb, Hubbard
>The Complete Homeowner. New York, Macmillan, 1965. 434 pp. $5.95 hardback.

Ulrey, Harry F.
>Builder's Encyclopedia. Indianapolis, Howard M. Sams & Co., 1970. 593 pp. $7.95 hardback.

### MASONRY & FIREPLACES

Building Research Institute of the National Academy of Sciences (publication #466). Modern Masonry; Natural Stone and Clay Products. Washington, 1956: 163 pp. $4.50 paperback.

Cement Mason's Manual for Residential Construction
Concrete Improvements for Farm and Ranch. 56¢
   Portland Cement Association
      Old Orchard Road
      Skokie, Illinois 60076

Dicker Stack Sack International
   2600 Fairmont Street
   Dallas, Texas 75201
   (Cement sack house construction data)

Huff, Darrell
      How to Work with Concrete and Masonry. New York, Harper & Row,
         1968. 179 pp. $2.50 paperback.
Orton, Vrest
      The Forgotten Art of Building a Fireplace. Dublin, NH, Yankee, 1969.
         60 pp. $2.00 paperback.
Sunset-Lane
      How to Plan and Build Your Fireplace. Menlo Park, CA, Sunset, 1972.
         112 pp. $1.95 paperback.
Wedge-Block, Inc.
   10439 Garibaldi
   St. Louis, MO 63131
   (tongue-in-groove bricks)


HANDYMAN & SHOP

Bacharach, Bert
      How to Do Almost Everything. New York, Simon & Schuster, 1970. 304
         pp. $6.95 hardback.
The Family Handyman Home Improvement Book. New York, Charles Scribner's
   Sons, 1973. 498 pp. $14.95 hardback.
Handyman Magazine
      Home Emergencies & Repairs. New York, Harper & Row. $6.95.
Manners, David X.
      Complete Book of Home Workshops. New York, Harper & Row, 1969.
         461 pp. $8.95 hardback.
O'Brien, Michael
      Demonstrating for Farm Mechanics. Danville, IL, The Interstate, 1957.
         242 pp. $5.50 hardback.

Schultz, Morton J.
    How to Fix It. New York, McGraw-Hill, 1971. 318 pp. $7.95 hard-
        back.
Wagner, Willis H.
    Modern Carpentry. South Holland, IL, Goodheart-Wilcox, 1969. 480 pp.
        $8.95 hardback.


PAINTING

Brushwell, William (Ed.)
    Goodheart-Wilcox's Painting and Decorating Encyclopedia. Homewood,
        IL, Goodheart-Wilcox, 1964. 288 pp. $6.40 hardback.


ELECTRICAL

Bredahl, A. Carl
    Home Wiring Manual. New York, McGraw-Hill, 1957. 221 pp. $7.50
        hardback.
Daniels, George
    How to be Your Own Home Electrician. New York, Harper & Row,
        1965. $2.50 paperback.
Mix, Floyd
    All About House Wiring. South Holland, IL, Goodheart-Wilcox, 1968.
        176 pp. $5.95 hardback.
Richter, H. P.
    Wiring Simplified. Minneapolis, MN 55408 (Box 8527, Lake St. Sta-
        tion), Park Publishing Company. $1.00.


PLUMBING (SEE CHAPTER 5 REFERENCES)


LOG CABINS

Angier, Bradford
    How to Build Your Home in the Woods. New York, Hart Publishing,
        1952. 300 pp. $2.95 paperback.
Building a Log House   50¢
    Cooperative Extension Service
    University of Alaska
    Box 1109
    Juneau, AL 99801

TIPIS

Laubin, Gladys & Reginald
    The Indian Tipi. New York, Ballantine, 1971. $1.65 paperback.
Brinton Bros.
  Wasichu Tipis
  East Sullivan, ME
Eepee Teepee Trading Co.
  260 S. Poteet Rd.
  Barrington, IL 60010
Goodwin-Cole Co.
  1315 Alhambra Boulevard
  Sacramento, CA 95816
Nomadics Tipi Makers
  Star Route, Box 41
  Cloverdale, OR 97112

YURTS

Home's Where Yurt (newsletter)
  Dawes Hill Commune
  Box 53
  West Danby, NY 14896
Yurt Construction Plan    $4.75
  Bill Coperthwaite
  Bucks Harbor, ME 04618

DOMES

Domebook 1    $4.00
Domebook 2    $4.20
  Shelter Publications
  Box 219
  Bolinas, CA 94924
Domecile Kit    $10.00
  Domecile Company
  P.O. Box 954
  Mendocino, CA
U.S. Plywood Corp.
  777 Third Avenue
  New York, NY 10017
  (plywood for domes)

## FOAM & PLASTICS

Architectural Research on Structural Potential of Foam Plastics for Housing in
   Underdeveloped Areas   $5.00
         Publication Distribution Service
         University of Michigan
         615 East University
         Ann Arbor, MI 48106
Skeist, Irving (Ed.)
         Plastics in Building. $20.00 hardback.
         Van Nostrand-Reinhold, 1966
            450 East 33rd Street
            New York, NY 10001
Lannon, Maurice
         Polyester and Fiberglass. Gem-O-Lite Plastics Corp., 5525 Cahuenga
         Blvd., North Hollywood, CA 91601, 1969. $4.50.
Futuro Modular House
   Futuro Corporation
   1900 Rittenhouse Square
   Philadelphia, PA 19103
Hutton, John
         Foam House Catalog, North Chichester, NH.


## FURNITURE

Hoard, F. E. & Marlow, A. W.
         Good Furniture You Can Make Yourself. New York, Collier, 1952.
         269 pp. $3.95 paperback.


## POLE CONSTRUCTION

American Wood Preservers Institute
   1651 Old Meadow Road
   McLean, VA 22101
   FHA (pole house construction)
Merrilees, Douglas & Loveday, Evelyn
         Pole Building Construction. Charlotte, VT, Garden Way, 1973. 48 pp.
         $3.00 paperback.


## EARTH

Earth for Homes: Ideas and Methods Exchange. $3.00 PB188918

Handbook for Building Domes of Earth. $3.00 PB179327
  Superintendent of Public Documents
  U.S. Government Printing Office
  Washington, DC 20402
Morse, Robert
  "Plastic B." 15–20 202nd Street, Bayside, NY 11360.

# TOOLS

Even if you don't build your own home, certain tools and skills will be necessary to maintain your homestead and for construction and repair of additional buildings. The prices listed here are approximations based on prices in the 1973 Montgomery Ward, Sears Roebuck and the NASCO Farm and Ranch Catalogues.

## CARPENTRY TOOLS—NON-POWERED

| | |
|---|---:|
| claw hammer | $ 5.00 |
| rip saw | 8–15.00 |
| cross-cut saw | 8–15.00 |
| tape measure | 4.00 |
| carpenter's rule | 2.50 |
| square | 2.50 |
| hand drill and bits | 10.00 |
| bubble level | 6.00 |
| keyhole saw | 3.50 |
| hack saw | 5.00 |
| set of chisels | 9.00 |
| putty knife | .89 |
| miter box | 4.00 |
| awl | 2.00 |
| set of files | 6.00 |
| paint brushes, 2", 4", 6" | 6–12.00 |
| block plane | 5.00 |
| extension ladder, wood | 40.00 |
| framing square | 8.00 |

## CARPENTRY TOOLS—POWERED

| | |
|---|---:|
| hand saw | 45–60.00 |
| table saw | 250.00 |
| electric drill & accessories | 10–60.00 |

# A HOMESTEAD IN CAMERA

Pictured by Charles Wicker and others on the following pages is the setting and the life of a modern family homestead. The location is New England, but the varieties of daily and seasonal activities, centered in working on and with the land, are much the same in many parts of America and Canada.

This is a life of near self-sufficiency. The order of work is matched to the growing crops, the homestead's animals, and to the demands and opportunities that nature provides in the slowly turning year. It is a life of work that is unremitting, yet which is naturally satisfying in its daily accomplishment. It is a life of security, harmony and self-fulfillment.

*As a bird would view it, the homestead, its fields, gardens and outbuildings nestle in a natural and efficient symmetry on the rolling land.* (P. COLEMAN)

*Now in mid-summer each day brings a new harvest ready to be picked for freezing, pickling and canning.* (P. COLEMAN)

*A heavy hay mulching of the garden area cuts the daily work to a minimum, and year by year helps build up the soil, too.* (P. COLEMAN)

*Some homesteaders favor milk goats when it comes to livestock. But here they swear by the family cow.*

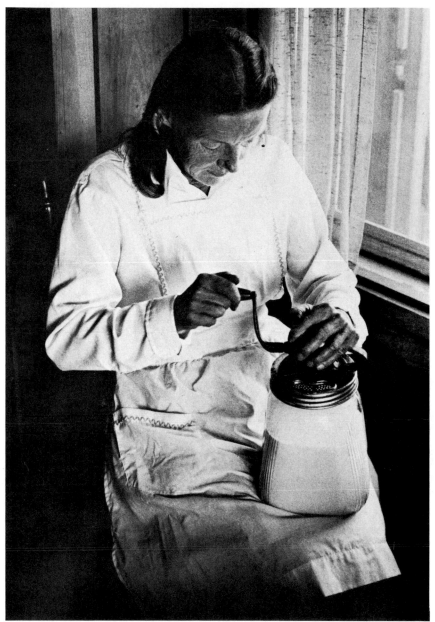

*Besides the cheeses to be made and stored, there are rich yields of butter to be won from the churn.*

*Few homesteads are without a flock of hens for ample supplies of eggs, and occasional chicken dinners.*

*A quarter-acre of wheat will provide all the fine flour a family needs in a year. If planted in the spring the full heads are golden brown by fall. Then it's gathered into shocks for threshing.*

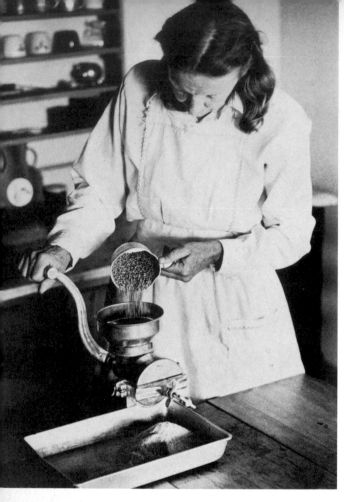

The wheat berries store perfectly
But the rich flour is perishable and
is ground for each baking. The
nutty flavored whole wheat loaves
need nothing with them but fresh
butter and wedges of cheddar
cheese.

*Spring lambs prosper on lush pasturage. A few on the homestead will provide fine meat and a bonus of wool for spinning and weaving.*

*The winter ahead demands working up an ample wood supply. A rented log-splitter saves valuable hours during the busy harvest season.*

The kitchen range will need kindling, too, and the splitting axe is the best tool to work it up.

*The big woodshed houses the many cords of seasoned hardwood needed for the winter, but a handy pile is always kept by the kitchen door.*

*Homestead life takes on [a]
slower pace in winter. N[ow]
there's time to read, to ma[ke]
clothing, do some fancy wo[rk]
or just to relax inside t[he]
snug and well-provision[ed]
home.*

# CHAPTER FOUR

# RAISING FOOD AND ANIMALS

One of the most important parts of homesteading (and one which can be followed even by people who do not consider themselves homesteaders), is raising your own food. On a basic level, this means supplementing your food supply from a home vegetable garden. It also may involve keeping dairy and meat animals and poultry if you have the space and inclination.

Though the savings on food costs are important, home gardening has other rewards as well. Home-grown vegetables are likely to be more nutritious and better tasting than those commercially sold. For another thing, gardening provides a certain independence from outside markets and cash demands. As food prices rise, more and more people are turning to home gardens as a healthful alternative.

"Growing your own" is not necessarily easy, especially for beginning gardeners who feel somewhat overwhelmed by how much there is to learn. However, it is perfectly possible to have a successful garden without prior experience. All you need is good soil, a little planning and a willingness to do the work involved in preparing the soil and cultivating.

## SOME GROUND RULES FOR BASIC GARDENING

So many good books are available about gardening that I shall not go into much detail here. Instead, what follows are some basic gardening principles, which you can augment from the chapter appendix. Essentially, gardening is only a matter of finding (or creating) fertile soil, planting seeds, protecting young plants from drought insects, disease and weeds, and harvesting your "crop" at the right time. You are simply encouraging plant growth by creating optimum conditions.

### PUT YOUR SOIL INTO SHAPE

The most important thing in gardening is to have *fertile soil*—soil that is healthy, well-balanced and easy to work. Most soils have certain deficiencies which must be corrected if plants are to have the best growth. These deficiencies can be discovered by a *soil test*, usually done free or at a nominal cost through your county agricultural office or state agricultural extension service. It is a good idea to have this test done before you even purchase a piece of land.

If your soil test shows a deficiency in one of the three basic elements—nitrogen, phosphorus or potash—you can correct it in various ways. Sometimes you will need to add only phosphate or only potash; other times you may be advised to add commercial fertilizer that is balanced (for instance, 5-10-15) for your general soil condition. If you are opposed to commercial fertilizer, you can use organic substances, such as cow or chicken manure, which is rich in nitrogen, or wood ashes, which are a good source of potash. In some way you want to make up any soil deficiency.

Some soils, of course, are worse than others, and may be made fertile only by the laborious and expensive addition over several years of tons of organic matter, manure or even imported topsoil. In such a case you may discover early that you do not want the land or that you must locate your garden elsewhere.

The most important element of fertile soil is *humus* or decayed organic matter. Good topsoil is rich in humus and represents years of natural decomposition of organic material. Without humus in the topsoil plants will be stunted and scrawny.

For this reason, building up the fertility of your soil mostly involves the addition of organic matter, usually in the form of *rotted barnyard manure* or *compost*. Barnyard manure is probably the best source of humus; cow manure, goat manure and poultry manure all are excellent. (This is one other good reason for keeping a few animals on the homestead.) Adding rotted manure also will help your soil hold moisture, will keep the soil loose, and will aid root development.

If you have no source of manure you can create decomposed organic matter for your garden by *composting* old leaves, weeds, grass clippings, straw, peat, domestic garbage and earth in a compost pile. This is a much slower method than using manure, since a compost pile may require a year or more before it is thoroughly decomposed.

To construct a compost pile, the plant refuse, earth (and if possible, manure), are piled in layers to a depth of three feet or so—deep enough that the pile will generate its own heat. The pile may be in a *compost bin* or simply stand alone; in any case it should be located in a shady area that is convenient to the garden. A compost pile must be watered every week or so, and occasionally turned to encourage uniform decomposition. Sometimes the addition of lime, or a nitrogenous fertilizer is recommended, as well as the covering of the pile with hay or black plastic. Other than that, composting is primarily a matter of waiting until the pile is finally broken down into humus.

The best information about your soil and its requirements can be obtained from your county agricultural agent or state extension service. Sometimes these services are also a source of free seeds or experimental plant varieties.

## LOCATE YOUR GARDEN WISELY

Choose a sunny spot for your garden that is fertile, well drained and convenient to the house. Do not plan a garden too close to trees, whose roots will rob your vegetables of the nutrients and moisture they need. The ideal location is a southern slope that is easily worked and harvested. Remember that killing frosts occur more often in low spots as the cold air tends to flow downhill. You sometimes can gain a few more days of gardening by locating your plot on a hillside or upland pasture.

The size of your garden is not arbitrary, but if you have had no experience, you should probably cultivate a small plot at first, perhaps 20 × 40 feet. A small garden well cared for produces more than a large one overrun with weeds.

## WORK THE SOIL

As you thoroughly spade or till the manure, fertilizer, or compost into your soil, be careful not to turn under your valuable topsoil. Deep plowing, for instance, will tend to do this and can be downright harmful, because it buries the organic matter which your plants will need. Instead, loosen the soil with a wheelhoe, disk harrow, or motor tiller that will not turn the topsoil under.

If you are starting a garden in sod, you have a different situation. The sod must be turned under completely. However, the answer is to plow deep in the fall, so that the sod can decompose and enrich the soil, as a fall spreading of manure will do. In the spring, another plowing will bring the topsoil back to the surface, where it can be worked with compost and fertilizer. If your garden soil isn't good, it may be best at first to use your manure and compost just in the rows and hills you plant to seed.

In readying the soil, pick out rocks and stones. Be sure that the soil is friable, loosely broken and finely smoothed before planting. This is hard work, to be sure, but careful soil preparation and the addition of rotted manure or compost will help you to produce superior garden vegetables on less land with less effort at cultivation. If you treat it right your garden soil will become better each year.

## PLAN AHEAD. BUY SUITABLE VARIETIES OF SEEDS AND PLANT ACCORDING TO DIRECTIONS

Seeds should be ordered from seed catalogs during the winter and a garden layout devised long before planting time. Doing so will avoid last-minute scurrying about for seeds and also will allow you to get some seedlings started indoors ahead of time. Talking to neighbors is a good way to find out what to plant in your area, what grows well here and to get other gardening tips. Plan to order the things your family likes, that are hardy in growth, and varieties good for winter storage.

A *garden plan* can be sketched out on paper, as shown here. Consider the available space, the kinds of vegetables you want, the plant heights, and the amount of sun and moisture required. Most gardening books give extensive details on seedling distances (plant and row), growing days required and the best soil and climate conditions.

In planting follow packet instructions about distances between plants and between rows, planting after frost danger is past. A small garden, for instance, may determine what vegetables you choose. You simply may not have enough room for something like pumpkins.

It is better to wait to plant rather than to take a chance on losing your young seedlings in a late frost or in cold wet soil when seeds may rot. Some things like peas and lettuce can go in early, however. Don't plant everything at once or you'll have too much of everything maturing at once. Plan *successive plantings* of things like beans, carrots and lettuce.

## CULTIVATE, WEED, MULCH, WATER

As your vegetables begin to come up, cultivate between the rows with a hoe. Pull out weeds by hand as they appear. Be careful not to disturb the roots of your garden plants by going too deep, of course.

# ½ ACRE GARDEN

| | | | |
|---|---|---|---|
| RASBERRIES | | | GRAPES |
| BLACKBERRIES | BERRIES | FRUITS | CURRANTS |
| BLUEBERRIES | | | GOOSEBERRIES |
| | PATH | | |
| STRAWBERRIES | | | ASPARAGUS |
| BROCCOLI | | | " |
| " | | | RHUBARB |
| CAULIFLOWER | | | POTATOES |
| CABBAGE | | | " |
| " | | | " |
| ONIONS | | | SQUASH |
| CHIVES | | | " |
| CORN | | | CORN |
| " | | | " |
| PEAS | | | SNOW PEAS |
| LETTUCE | | | POLE BEANS |
| TOMATOES | | | BUSH BEANS |
| SPINACH | VEGETABLES | VEGETABLES | CHARD |
| CARROTS | | | SALSIFY |
| TURNIPS | | | BEETS |
| PEPPERS | | | CHARD |
| SHALLOTS | | | EGGPLANT |
| HERBS | | | HERBS |

Once your plants are large enough, you can save labor by laying down a mulch of paper, hay or of plastic around the plants. This will help to keep moisture in and to keep down weeds. An organic mulch of hay or barn bedding is fine, and it becomes part of the soil later. But for this reason some gardeners prefer a plastic mulch that does not have to be frequently renewed.

Unless you live in a semi-desert area your garden will not need too much watering. A good soaking every ten days is sufficient, better than frequent light sprinklings which barely penetrate the surface. Soil that is wet, of course, cannot be cultivated until the surface dries out.

## KEEP DOWN PESTS

Two kinds of pests are likely to threaten your tender sprouts—*animals,* such as woodchucks, rabbits or deer (as well as stray cows) and *insects,* such as cutworms, aphids or beetles. A woodchuck can do a tremendous amount of damage and so can a deer—probably more damage in a night than all the insect pests in an entire season. If you have a potential deer or rabbit problem, a *high* chicken wire fence will keep them out (remember that a deer can jump a six-foot fence easily). Woodchucks are more difficult, but if they are a real menace they can be poisoned or shot. Sometimes a dog on the premises is the best deterrent.

Insect pests are more tricky. The commercial answer, insecticides, work quite well at eliminating harmful insects. But unfortunately they also eliminate friendly insects and leave a poisonous residue on fruits and vegetables—a side effect that most people would like to avoid.

Some alternatives to insecticides include building up soil *fertility,* setting up simple *mechanical devices* to thwart insects, and introducing *insect "allies"* that are natural enemies to the harmful pests. The first alternative is based on the recognition that plants grown in healthy, fertile soil better resist disease and insects; they are unlikely to suffer damage if your soil is well-balanced and your plants healthy to start with. There are safe organic remedies, too (see chapter appendix). Simple devices such as pa-

per collars are effective against cutworms, for instance, and other types of arrangements will reduce insect damage.

Birds, lady bugs and preying mantises are a few of the many natural predators of harmful garden insects. By introducing natural enemies, you often can reduce substantially the population of your most bothersome pests without killing friends and foes alike.

Finally, there are the *companion plants* which help each other or repel certain pests (see chapter appendix).

### HARVEST WHEN PLANTS ARE TENDER

As crops begin to ripen, inspect your garden daily. Pick vegetables that are young and tender; they will taste better than older, larger ones. For the very best taste, pick your vegetables just before using. Selecting tender, fresh-picked plants is especially important for canning or freezing. If done properly, canned and frozen vegetables and fruit taste almost like fresh, and retain most of the nutrients.

### KEEP YOUR GARDEN PLANTED IN "GREEN MANURE"

After your last vegetables are out of the ground in the early fall, work up the soil again and plant a quick cover crop like rye grass. When you are ready to plant in the spring, work this green compost into the topsoil. It will decay quickly and provide much additional organic material for your young plants.

## EXTENDING YOUR GROWING SEASON

There are a couple of ways you can extend your growing season, so as to enjoy fresh vegetables from May to December even in the north country. One way, as mentioned earlier, is to locate your garden on an upland slope. Frosts are less likely on higher sloping land, and you can gain a few days or weeks on growing time.

Another way is to get a headstart by starting seeds indoors or outside in a hotbed or coldframe. These structures are quite similar—both are

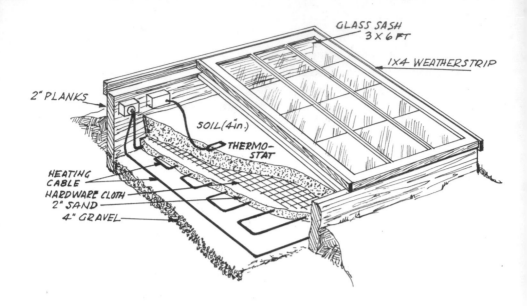

GLASS SASH 3 X 6 FT

1X4 WEATHERSTRIP

2" PLANKS

SOIL (4 in.)

THERMO-STAT

HEATING CABLE
HARDWARE CLOTH
2" SAND
4" GRAVEL

sort of miniature greenhouses. The difference (see sketch) is that a cold-frame is heated only by sunlight, while a hotbed is heated artificially by decomposing manure or heat cables or pipes.

As shown here, a ~~coldframe~~ is simply a shallow box with a sloping glass cover that can be raised to get at the seedlings (or to reduce interior heat). In a coldframe, seedlings can be started outside while snow is still on the ground, since they are protected at night by rug coverings and earth or leaves banked around the sides. During the day, you remove the coverings and let the seedlings enjoy their own little greenhouse. Plants started in this fashion can be transplanted to the garden later, when the weather is warm enough.

A ~~hotbed~~ heated by manure gives you even more freedom to your gardening. However, when the manure stops decomposing it stops producing heat, and a fresh load must be provided periodically (with resulting movement of the hotbed and plants). Other methods of heating a hotbed that do not have this drawback include buried electric heat cables, a connection from the hotbed to the cellar window or a special furnace pipe. If you do not have a large freezer you may want to investigate hotbeds further; otherwise you may find it as satisfactory to rely on fresh-frozen vegetables from your summer garden.

You may want to go into indoor gardening under lights, or (though expensive to build and operate) your own walk-in *greenhouse*. A real greenhouse can be very satisfying for the avid gardener, and it certainly makes much easier the raising of seedlings and house plants. But a projecting window in the harvest room that is set aside for seedlings, as described in Chapter Three, will be a cheaper solution.

## BERRIES AND GRAPES

Another part of gardening that many people overlook is a berry patch and vineyard. In terms of work and costs, berries and grapes are among the best garden investments. Bush berries, for instance, require very little work, can be planned to ripen successively from June to October, and can be easily frozen and enjoyed all winter. The only real labor involved is pruning and mulching and sometimes providing plant supports. For more information visit a local nursery (and see chapter appendix).

Grapes are easy to grow, too, and may provide the incentive to making your own home wines. The important thing in wine-making is to buy the right grapevines and to be patient, since they take up to four years to bear fruit. There are many books out about home wine-making. Especially good is S. M. Tritton's "Amateur Wine Making."

## FRUIT TREES

Besides a vegetable garden and berry patch, you probably will want to start a home orchard of fruit and nut trees. By doing so, you will eventually be able to provide yourself with all the nuts, apples, pears, cherries, plums or peaches that your homestead can use and perhaps have some to trade or sell.

If you have just bought land and plan to have an orchard, it's best to put it in the first spring—perhaps even before building your house. That will reduce your two- or three-year waiting time for fruit to a minimum. Also, read up on fruit and nut trees before buying and decide on the varieties best for your climate and the number of trees your homestead can use.

Besides different fruit, you have a choice of *standard, semi-dwarf* or *dwarf* trees. Dwarf trees are much smaller than normal, but they bear

|  | Distance Apart | | Amount of seed, or no. of plants per 50-foot row |
| Kinds | Rows, feet | Plants in rows, inches | |
| --- | --- | --- | --- |
| Bean (bush) | 2 | 2 to 3 | 4 oz. |
| (pole) | 2 | 8 to 12 | 4 oz. |
| Beet | 1½ to 2 | 1 to 3 | ½ oz. |
| Broccoli Early | 2½ | 18 | 1 pkt. |
| Late | 2½ | 18 | 1 pkt. |
| Cabbage Early | 2½ | 18 | 1 pkt. |
| Late | 2½ | 18 | 1 pkt. |
| Carrot | 1½ to 2 | 1 to 2 | ¼ oz. |
| Cauliflower | 2½ | 18 | 1 pkt. |
| Chard, Swiss | 2 | 8 to 12 | ½ oz. |
| Chinese Cabbage | 2 | 12 | 1 pkt. |
| Corn | 2½ to 3 | 12 to 18 | 2 oz. |
| Cucumber Slicing | 4 | 12 to 24 | ⅛ oz. |
| Pickling | 4 | 12 to 24 | ⅛ oz. |
| Endive | 2 | 8 to 12 | 1 pkt. |
| Herbs | 2 | 6 | 1 pkt. |
| Lettuce (leaf) | 1½ | 6 | 1 pkt. |
| (head) | 1½ | 12 | 1 pkt. |
| Muskmelon | 4 | 12 to 24 | 1 pkt. |
| Onion Transplants | 1½ | 3 | 1 pkt. |
| Seed or sets | 1½ | 2 to 3 | 1 pkt. seed, 1½ lb. sets |
| New Zealand Spinach | 2 to 3 | 24 to 36 | 1 oz. |
| Parsnip | 1½ to 2 | 2 to 4 | ¼ oz. |
| Pea | 1½ to 3 | 2 | 4 oz. |
| Pumpkin | 6 to 8 | 36 to 48 | 1 oz. |
| Radish (spring and fall crop) | 1 | 1 | ½ oz. |
| Rutabaga | 2 | 6 | ½ oz. |
| Spinach (spring and fall crop) | 1½ | 4 to 6 | ½ oz. |
| Squash | 6 to 8 | 36 to 48 | 1 oz. |
| Tomato Staked | 2 | 18 to 24 | 25 to 33 plants |
| Unstaked | 3 | 36 | 17 plants |
| Turnip | 1½ to 2 | 3 to 4 | ½ oz. |
| Watermelon | 4 to 6 | 12 to 24 | ½ oz. |

| Depth to cover, inches | No. of days seeding to harvest | Approximate yield per 50-foot row | How to use or store |
|---|---|---|---|
| 1½ to 2 | 52 to 70 | 30 to 50 | Fresh, fresh frozen, canned, |
| 1½ to 2 | 65 to 75 | qt. | pickled |
| ½ | 55 to 70 | 250 roots | Fresh, pickled, canned, cool cellar |
| Transplants | 60 to 80 | 30 to 40 | Fresh, fresh frozen |
| ½ | | qt. | |
| Transplants | 60 to 80 | 30 heads | Fresh, raw |
| ½ | 100 to 105 | 30 heads | Fresh, raw, kraut, or storage |
| ½ | 60 to 75 | 30 to 75 lb. | Fresh, raw, canned, cool cellar |
| Transplants | 60 to 80 | 30 heads | Fresh, fresh frozen |
| ½ | 50 to 60 | Use all season | Fresh |
| ½ | 70 to 90 | 50 heads | Fresh |
| 1 to 2 | 70 to 100 | 45 to 75 ears | Fresh, fresh frozen, canned |
| ½ to 1 | 65 to 75 | 100 to 150 | Raw |
| ½ to 1 | 60 to 70 | 50 to 150 fruits | Pickled |
| ¼ | 70 to 90 | | Salad |
| ¼ | | | |
| ¼ | 40 to 50 | 100 | Raw |
| ¼ | 70 to 75 | 50 heads | Raw |
| ½ | 70 to 100 | 75 to 150 | Fresh |
| Transplants | 115 to 135 | 50 to 75 lb. | Raw, fresh, dry dark cool storage |
| Seed ½ | 95 | | |
| Sets 1 | | | |
| ½ | 60 to 80 | Use all season | Fresh |
| ½ | 120 to 150 | 150 to 300 roots | Store sand, moss, sawdust; or leave in ground over winter |
| 1½ to 2 | 60 to 80 | 20 to 40 qt. pods | Fresh, fresh frozen, canned |
| 1 | 110 to 130 | 30 to 50 fruits | Fresh, store dry |
| ¼ | 25 to 35 | 30 to 100 bunches | Fresh |
| ¼ | 110 to 130 | 100 lb. | Fresh, stored |
| ½ | 40 to 45 | 1 to 2 bu. | Fresh, fresh frozen |
| 1 | 90 to 115 | 100 fruits | Fresh, store dry |
| Transplants | 100 to 130 | 150 to 300 | Fresh, canned |
| Transplants | 100 to 130 | 150 to 300 fruits | Fresh, canned |
| ¼ | 50 to 70 | 150 roots | Fresh |
| 1 | 90 to 100 | 75 to 100 fruits | Fresh |

normal size fruit. They also bear fruit in a shorter time than standard trees, as you can see from the comparison chart shown here.

## FRUIT TREE COMPARISON CHART

| | YEARS AFTER PLANTING TO FIRST FRUITING | | ORCHARD SPACING | |
| | *Standard* | *Dwarf* | *Standard* | *Dwarf* |
|---|---|---|---|---|
| Apple | 6-8 | 2-4 | 40′ x 40′ | 8′ x 10′ |
| Pear | 5-7 | 2 | 20′ x 20′ | 10′ x 10′ |
| Sweet Cherry | 6-7 | 4-5 | 25′ x 25′ | 12′ x 12′ |
| Sour Cherry | 4 | 3 | 20′ x 20′ | 12′ x 12′ |
| Plum (Japanese) | 4-5 | 3 | 20′ x 20′ | 12′ x 12′ |
| Plum (European) | 4-5 | 4 | 20′ x 20′ | 12′ x 12′ |
| Quince | 5-6 | 4 | 15′ x 15′ | 10′ x 10′ |
| Nectarine | 3 | 2 | 20′ x 20′ | 12′ x 12′ |
| Apricot | 3 | 3 | 20′ x 20′ | 12′ x 12′ |
| Peach | 3 | 2 | 20′ x 20′ | 12′ x 12′ |

Among the other advantages to dwarf trees are the ease in pruning, spraying and harvesting, the reduced amount of damaged fruit because of the shorter fall distance, and the greater variety possible in a home orchard by having more trees in a limited space.

The only disadvantages of dwarf trees are their somewhat higher cost over standard trees and their shorter life—25 or 30 years compared with 40 or more for a standard tree.

Much care should be taken in planting and maintaining your orchard, including yearly pruning and perhaps spraying. A good book to read for more information is *Dwarf Fruit Trees for the Home Gardener,* by Lawrence Southwick. Considering their relatively small expense, fruit trees are a good investment. Not only will they provide you with years of delicious fruit, but they will increase the value of your property by many times their cost.

## GARDENING ECONOMICS

Although gardening certainly can be done very cheaply, it is also possible to spend a surprising amount of money to begin raising vegetables. The purchase of a garden tractor or tiller, for instance, may involve several hundred dollars. Even without such mechanical help, cash expenses will include spades, hoe, pruners, perhaps a wheel hoe, fork, wheelbarrow or garden cart, trowel, string, plastic sheeting and seeds. You may find that your garden is simply not a profitable enterprise the first season. But the basic tools, of course, will last for many years with proper care, and are a capital investment toward your gardening business. Your garden, remember, can be your largest single effort toward homestead self-sufficiency.

## HOME STORAGE OF FRUITS AND VEGETABLES

To save money on food all year round it is important to preserve much of the garden vegetables and fruits that you harvest during the summer and fall. There are many methods of doing so, some ancient and some modern, from root cellar storage to freezing. The efforts of the harvest often are frantic enough without wondering *how,* so decide in advance which of the following methods best suits your climate, your facilities, and your taste, and which is best for each crop—for instance, canning tomatoes, freezing strawberries and dry storing cabbages.

### COMMON STORAGE

Some fruits and vegetables can be stored successfully in cool, dark places. This works well for roots, apples, pears, celery and cabbage, to name a few. The most obvious places for such storage are an old cellar or the earth itself, and there are many variations possible for each. Carefully-constructed root cellars, for instance, often are found in old farmhouses and they can be built into new houses. Earth-covered barrels, boxes or mounds can be devised for outside storage. Or some root crops can be left until spring in the earth where they grew, insulated with mulch. Some crops, like parsnips and leeks even are preferred after being allowed to freeze in the ground and for harvesting in the spring. Common storage is

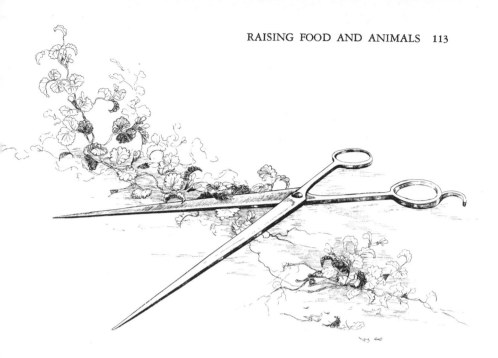

inexpensive; and if the vegetables are stored properly they can be enjoyed all through the winter.

## DRYING

Drying is not so popular as other storage methods, but it is a perfectly good way to preserve apples, corn, beans, peas and herbs. You will probably have to experiment to discover what fruits you prefer dried. Drying does not affect A and B vitamins much, but it does tend to destroy vitamin C. It is also a fairly time-consuming process, whether you use the sun or drying racks (it takes about 10-12 hours) for fruit and moist vegetables. Still, drying is a cheap way to store some foods, and like common storage it usually does not require electrical power or expensive machinery. Drying and smoking of meats is often useful, too.

## CURING AND SALTING

Salting is one of the oldest methods of preserving food, particularly meats and fish. In vegetables large amounts of salt inhibit the growth of bacteria but produce a very salty product that must be freshened, thereby washing away some of the nutrients. *Small* amounts of salt cause fermentation, the process for making pickles, sauerkraut and for using green tomatoes. Because they do not have to be soaked to remove excess salt, they retain much of their food value. Salting is a cheap method of preservation and may be appropriate for some of your garden produce, though it is more applicable for meats, sometimes combined with smoking.

CANNING

Canning in glass jars has been the standard method for food preservation until fairly recently. Canning involves the heating of both vegetable and container to kill bacteria, followed by a cooling period that sets the jar seal. It is essential in home canning to follow directions carefully, since it is possible to get botulism poisoning from improperly canned products. (The botulism organism grows in the *absence* of air only.) Proper canning procedure completely eliminates this danger.

Canned vegetables tend to lose some of their vitamin value during storage, but they retain the most possible if all the juices are used in heating and serving. Canning is certainly best for tomatoes and for some other vegetables.

Canning equipment requires more financial outlay than common storage, drying or salting, but the expense is spread over a long period of time. Canning still is a lot less expensive than freezing.

FREEZING

Freezing is the simplest and easiest way to preserve food. In addition frozen foods retain high amounts of all their nutrients and taste most like fresh. Homesteaders today probably rely more on freezing than on any other method of keeping food, unless they live without electricity.

The only major drawback to freezing is the high cost of a freezer and the possibility of a prolonged power failure, which could ruin an entire season's worth of vegetables or hundreds of pounds of meat. There is really no way to avoid the cost of a freezer and it will, after all, be spread over many years. There *are* ways to avoid the consequences of a power failure, such as the use of dry ice (if you can get it) to maintain freezer temperature, and having a standby home electric generator for just such emergencies.

There are, of course, some vegetables that simply cannot be frozen, such as lettuce, cucumbers, celery and radishes. These salad vegetables and some others are best suited to some form of common storage, or must be used fresh.

Here are a few general rules for homestead food preservation:

1. Use fresh products picked in their prime.
2. Store all canned, dried or raw produce in a cool, dry place.
3. For freezing, canning or drying, preserve the foods immediately after picking, before they lose their quality and vitamins. Follow the particular rules for each process carefully.
4. Vegetables and fruits that are to be stored raw must be absolutely free of all decay or cuts. Handle your produce as though they were eggs in order not to bruise them. The old saying that one rotten apple can spoil a barrel is literally true.
5. Eat all home-stored produce within a year.

Your food storage problems and solutions of course will depend on where you live. In a warm climate you may be able to grow fresh vegetables all year round, using refrigeration only for keeping meat. If you have special problems, you may find original solutions of your own, as pioneer homesteaders often were forced to do.

There are several good books that give detailed advice and directions about food storage (see chapter appendix). For more information consult them and your neighbors.

## WILD FOODS

If you live in a rural area there are certain to be many nearby places that are good sources of wild food. Wild fruits and other plants may constitute an occasional saving on food—and they are fun to find. Wild strawberries, apples, blueberries, pears and blackberries are common in many parts of the United States in the summer. Watercress and mint are easily found, and in marshy areas, cattail and sometimes wild rice. Often wild nuts—hickory, butternuts, beech, pine, hazelnuts and acorns—are

## FREEZING POINTS, RECOMMENDED STORAGE CONDITIONS, AND LENGTH OF STORAGE PERIOD OF VEGETABLES AND FRUITS

| Commodity | Freezing Point °F. | Place to Store |
|---|---|---|
| Vegetables: | | |
| Dry beans and peas | | Any cool, dry place |
| Late cabbage | 30.4 | Pit, trench, or outdoor cellar |
| Cauliflower | 30.3 | Storage cellar |
| Late celery | 31.6 | Pit or trench; roots in soil in storage cellar. |
| Endive | 31.9 | Roots in soil in storage cellar |
| Onions | 30.6 | Any cool, dry place |
| Parsnips | 30.4 | Where they grew, or in storage cellar. |
| Peppers | 30.7 | Unheated basement or room |
| Potatoes | 30.9 | Pit or in storage cellar |
| Pumpkins and squashes | 30.5 | Home cellar or basement |
| Root crops (miscellaneous). | | Pit or in storage cellar |
| Sweet potatoes | 29.7 | Home cellar or basement |
| Tomatoes (mature, green). | 31.0 | Same as above. |
| Fruits: | | |
| Apples | 29.0 | Fruit storage cellar |
| Grapefruit | 29.8 | Same as above. |
| Grapes | 28.1 | Same as above. |
| Oranges | 30.5 | Same as above. |
| Pears | 29.2 | Same as above. |

| STORAGE CONDITIONS | | Length of |
| --- | --- | --- |
| *Temperature* | *Humidity* | *Storage Period* |
| °F. | | |
| 32° to 40° | Dry | As long as desired. |
| Near 32° as possible | Moderately moist. | Through late fall and winter. |
| Same as above. | Same as above. | 6 to 8 weeks. |
| Same as above. | Same as above. | Through late fall and winter. |
| Same as above. | Same as above. | 2 to 3 months. |
| Same as above. | Dry | Through fall and winter. |
| Same as above. | Moist | Same as above. |
| 45° to 50° | Moderately moist. | 2 to 3 weeks. |
| 35° to 40° | Same as above. | Through fall and winter. |
| 55° | Moderately dry. | Same as above. |
| Near 32° as possible | Moist | Same as above. |
| 55° to 60° | Moderately dry. | Same as above. |
| 55° to 70° | Same as above. | 4 to 6 weeks. |
| Near 32° as possible | Moderately moist. | Through fall and winter. |
| Same as above. | Same as above. | 4 to 6 weeks. |
| Same as above. | Same as above. | 1 to 2 months. |
| Same as above. | Same as above. | 4 to 6 weeks. |
| Same as above. | Same as above. | 4 to 6 weeks. |

available in abundance. You can find wild asparagus and mushrooms—the list could go on and on.

But as a *regular* source of food, wild plants probably are not worth the time it takes to find them. For the busy homesteader they have to remain an occasional and exciting addition to his regular food supply. But this shouldn't deter you from watching for unusual sources of wild food and adding them to the home menu. Time-consuming also but often more worthwhile to supplement the meat larder is hunting and fishing.

## ANIMALS ON THE HOMESTEAD

Vegetables are basic, and many homesteaders such as the Nearings choose to make vegetables their main diet. Others, however, want to produce their own eggs, milk and meat right on the homestead.

Keeping birds and animals of any kind is a definite responsibility. They require proper housing, regular feeding and a food supply, and occasional veterinary care. You certainly should consider carefully whether you are ready to provide the necessary care and feeding before you begin adding animals to your small homestead.

Before getting into animals, you need to consider especially the initial costs involved. While it may eventually pay to have hens, ducks, goats, veal calves, lambs, pigs, geese or bees, these are separate investments that may take months or sometimes years to turn to a profit. You must be able to make the initial investment fairly painlessly; otherwise you will be constantly worrying about the very enterprises that were supposed to give you security. For this reason it is best to add animals to your homestead gradually as you get others on a paying basis.

Some animal enterprises, of course, are much easier and less expensive than others. A few geese or hens will not cost too much to buy, house and feed, especially if you buy pullets or goslings and raise them. Keeping dairy animals, on the other hand, requires a much larger expense in purchasing animals, fencing, shelter and feed. They take more time, too.

Apart from the basic cost of housing and initial purchase, you should consider the period of animal growth to maturity and the accompanying feed costs. While raising a few chickens to egg laying or eating age is inexpensive, the same can hardly be said about raising a calf 2½ years to milking age.

An important final factor is how much land you have. If your pasture is limited, it probably would not be profitable for you to have a cow or steer. A better bet would be goats, rabbits, geese or similar animals that do not require much grazing land. Here are some brief notes on different homestead animals and the basic considerations in keeping them.

## THE CHICKEN AND THE EGG

For a small family of three or four the eggs produced by a half dozen hens probably are plenty. For $50-100, you can buy or build a suitable small henhouse that will provide the necessary four to five square feet of floor space needed per bird. Henhouse kits also are available and are often advertised in poultry magazines. The important thing is that the house be sunny, well ventilated and not damp or drafty.

If you plan to buy much commercial feed for your hens, you may find that the feed expense and time of keeping hens will make your eggs almost as expensive as those store bought. Check feed prices beforehand and figure what your costs will be. If you can raise some of the feed (such as skim milk from a cow), you are more likely to come out ahead. In the long run, the costs of having your own laying hens probably are less.

The arrangement of a chicken house, the breed of hen, feeding techniques and prevention of disease all are topics that you can learn about from poultry books or from your neighbors. A good book to begin with is *Starting Right with Poultry,* by G. T. Klein.

Besides having your own eggs you may want to raise eating chickens (broilers). The initial expense is about the same as for laying hens—you need a *brooder* (a warm box for young chicks) and some sort of small poultry run. Less space is needed for broilers (especially while chicks), since birds raised in confinement for two months will be much tenderer than chickens allowed to range.

The feed expense for broilers is higher in confinement because they do not forage and need vitamin-fortified feed. However, they require little space and can save you dollars on meat bills, depending on market prices.

As poultry books will tell you, a very important thing in raising chickens is to keep the poultry house clean and the birds free from disease. Equally important are not overcrowding the birds and keeping the young chicks away from older hens. By following the advice found in a good poultry book or learned from an experienced neighbor you should be able to save a good amount on eggs and eating chickens within a year.


## DAIRY ANIMALS

Depending on your diet you actually may save as much food money by keeping dairy animals as by cultivating a large garden. Milk, butter, cheese and ice cream are expensive items in most stores and constitute up to 25 percent of some food budgets. For this reason alone, it is worth your time to consider keeping a family cow or milk goats.

Although a cow is familiar to more people, many homesteaders choose instead to keep milk goats. Each has its advantages, and your choice must

depend on how much milk you can use and what sort (and amount) of pasture land you have. Here is a brief comparison of goats and cows:

| | *1 cow* | *2 goats* |
|---|---|---|
| milk produced daily | 10–15 qts. | 3–7 quarts |
| pasture needed | 1–2 acres | less than 1 acre |
| feed used per year | 2 tons hay | 1200 lbs. hay |
| | 1 ton grain | ½ ton grain |

As you can see from this that a cow gives much more milk, eats more hay and grain, and needs more (and better) pasture. A cow also is likely to cost more than two goats, though this is variable. A cow will require more fencing, but will not need so strong a fence.

Two goats will produce less milk, which might be appealing to a small family, and they will eat much less hay and grain. They require less pasture and thrive on brush and shrubs. Goat fencing must be high and strong, for goats are agile jumpers. Goats also are easier to transport when breeding time comes. (A goat fits conveniently into the back seat of a small car.)

Except for being slightly whiter, goat's milk is indistinguishable from cow's milk. However, the cream separates much more slowly and must be extracted by a separator. The milking time is probably a little less for two goats. Both a cow and goat will provide excellent manure for the garden, and they probably will have about the same veterinary bills.

Whichever you choose, dairy animals are a real responsibility: they must be fed and milked twice a day, month in and month out. They require a barn, pasture land, space for feed storage, milk processing equipment and various other barn implements. Over several years, of course, a cow or goats will save you hundreds of dollars in food costs, but initially you must be prepared to make a cash investment of $500–600 (less if you can adapt a barn very cheaply).

### SAVE ON FEED—GROW YOUR OWN

The best way to make animals pay on the homestead is to raise both the animals and their feed. This means having some acreage to hay, some in grain or corn and some in root vegetables such as turnips or sugar beets. To some extent garden roughage, beets, and turnips can be substituted for commercial grain, with perhaps a slight loss in milk quantity.

### THE USEFULNESS OF A SMALL BARN

The biggest expense in fitting out to keep animals is housing—a cow stable, henhouse, goat shed or geese hut. All have to be provided in some way or another, though none of these need be elaborate. Two goats, for instance, will do fine in a 6 × 10 shed.

The most economical housing arrangement may be that suggested in the *"Have-More" Plan*—a small barn that houses hens, rabbits, goats, sheep. This ideal small barn might cost $500 more or less, depending on how elaborate you make it. Having all your animals under one roof saves the duplicated expense of several smaller buildings and cuts down on chore time proportionately. It simply requires careful planning for light, pens, water, feeding arrangements and feed storage—all of which will save you time in the future. For more information, read the *"Have-More" Plan* section on small barns.

## MEAT ANIMALS

### GEESE

Geese are among the cheapest and easiest of poultry to raise. They require no fancy house—just a simple three-sided shelter for very bad weather. A fence 36 inches high is easily sufficient. Geese make their own nests and hatch their own eggs—and they don't require a pond.

Americans do not think of geese much as eating birds for some reason, but remember the inevitable Christmas goose in England? Geese are fully as delicious as turkeys and can be cheaply raised from day-old eggs by a broody hen.

Other advantages to geese are their fearlessness—which protects them from attack by dogs, cats or rats—and their noise. A honking goose in the suburbs may not be everybody's favorite, but it makes a good watch-dog in the country. Geese are friendly and will follow you around the yard.

Besides their meat, geese are valuable for their feathers (goose down), for their fat and for their livers, which are rich in vitamin A.

## DUCKS

If you have a small pond or stream, ducks are another easy bird to raise. Not only are they good for the table, but duck eggs are delicious, too. Ducks can be raised from ducklings, hatched from eggs by your hens or bought full-grown. They multiply rapidly: a trio can produce up to 25 ducklings in six months.

Unlike geese, ducks do need some sort of house, such as the small coop with door. They will build their own nests and hatch ducklings about twice a year.

Of the several breeds, Muscovy ducks are the quietest and most apt to hatch their eggs. They are "fliers," though, and require either high fencing or the clipping of wingtip feathers.

## VEAL CALVES

Veal is simply calf meat. If you have a family cow she will have a calf periodically and you will find yourself selling or raising a calf anyway. You might as well make it a good veal calf.

For the best veal a calf should be fed four to five quarts of milk a day until he is eight weeks old, then slaughtered. The calf's use of his mother's milk will not interfere with your family milk supply much, because at that point the cow will be producing up to 16 quarts a day.

Another source of veal is to buy an unwanted calf from a local dairyman when it is a week or two old and fatten it yourself until it is eight weeks old. You'll still save a good deal.

## BEEF STEER

To avoid paying commercial beef prices you might consider raising a steer on your own land. All you need is an acre or so of pasture and enough hay (two acres of clover or alfalfa is ideal). Shelter need be only a simple three-sided shed, and if you can set up a source of water your work will be minimal.

Such a calf can be fattened as long as you wish, though the most economical arrangement probably is to buy the calf in the spring and put him to pasture for the summer and fall, adding grain feed to fatten him for slaughter in November.

One advantage to pasturing a steer is that a single strand of electric fencing is enough to hold him. Combined with a home freezer, it is entirely feasible for a family to raise a beef steer and freeze several hundred pounds of beef—perhaps more than enough for the whole year. Probably the best plan is to divide your beef with a neighbor, slaughtering your steer one year and his the next.

## RABBITS

Rabbits can be bred as meat animals without much difficulty if you can regard them as meat and not as pets. You simply need a half dozen wire rabbit hutches, a buck rabbit and a couple of does.

Rabbits prefer root vegetables like carrots, but also should be fed alfalfa or clover hay and vegetable parings. Prepared pellet foods or whole grain also are good supplements.

Rabbits are especially well suited to a small place because they take up little room (3 × 10 feet is plenty). They are inexpensive, quiet and can be raised ready to eat in ten weeks or so. Rabbits can stand plenty of cold, though damp or hot weather bothers them.

## PIGS

Pigs are useful animals for the small homestead for several reasons. They are easily fattened in confinement, provide a tremendous amount of meat for the expense, and do not require complicated or expensive housing.

A six- or seven-week-old pig can be bought for perhaps $20 in April, fattened (a pig will gain a pound a day) through the summer and fall, and slaughtered in December at about 225 lbs. He will provide some 55 lbs. of ham, 40 lbs. of bacon and sausage, lard and other things besides— easily enough for a family of three or four.

The important thing is to take care in buying your piglet. Choose one that is long-bodied, and buy from a good breeder or reputable farmer. The old saying is that the day you buy your pig is the day you make or lose the most money (see chapter appendix).

SHEEP

A few sheep fit into some homesteads for their value as spring lamb more than wool. But lambs require expensive fencing and supervision. They need little feed besides good pasture. Read about them in *Starting Right With Sheep*.

## OTHER HOMESTEAD PRODUCTS

BEES

Many people are reluctant to add bees to their small homestead because they don't know anything about managing them and are afraid of getting stung. However, as Ed Robinson points out in the *"Have-More" Plan*, you won't get stung if you handle bees properly, and the only real way to learn is to get some.

A bee hive takes only a few hours of work a year and can produce 75 lbs. of honey or more. That undoubtedly is enough for a small homestead and probably would enable you to sell some. Most states require inspection and licensing, however, for the sale of honey.

There has been a huge increase in the demand for honey in the last few years, and as a result bees are difficult to buy. Most beekeepers are meeting the honey market by expanding their hives rather than selling the new swarms. If you can get bees somehow, it is a good idea. Your original hive will expand to several as you get new swarms, and for your original in-

vestment you'll soon have more honey than you can use (see chapter appendix).

FISH

You may remember from Chapter Three that a swampy pasture area was excavated to create a pond, as shown in the homestead layout. Besides providing water for livestock, such a pond can be stocked to supply you with your own fresh fish. The trick is simply to get a "food chain" started by stimulating the growth of algae, which will feed small sunfish, which in turn will feed bass or other pan species. Once the algae is there all you need to do is stock the pond. To keep the food chain in operation, continue to "fertilize" the algae—and do plenty of fishing. A farm pond has other valuable uses, too. Among them are water for ducks and geese, swimming, skating and fire protection.

HOMEMADE WINE

As mentioned earlier, a home vineyard can be a fine source of grapes for home wine-making. If you have a well-equipped harvest kitchen, you will find yourself thinking about making wine, cider and many other products you have never tried to make before.

# SUMMARY

One of the most important parts of homesteading is reducing your cash needs and increasing your self-sufficiency by raising most of your own food. To do so, however, you will have to make the necessary investments in working your soil, planting and weeding your garden, and preserving your vegetable "harvest."

Similarly, to enjoy home-raised animal products, you will have to be able to lay out the initial capital for dairy or meat animals, a small barn or other livestock housing, grain and feed, and fencing. Rather than try too many ventures, you are likely to want one or two animals in addition to your garden, adding others only as you can afford to do so.

By choosing a garden and animals that fit your needs and your budget, however, you will eventually enjoy the many ways that a productive homestead gives you delicious fruit, vegetables and meats at a fraction of their commercial cost.

# APPENDIX

## SUGGESTED READING

### GARDENING ENCYCLOPEDIAS

Taylor, Norman
   Taylor's Encyclopedia of Gardening. Boston, Houghton Mifflin, 1961.
      1329 pp. $12.96 hardback.
Seymour, E. L. D: (Ed.)
   The Wise Garden Encyclopedia. New York, Grosset & Dunlap, 1970.
      1380 pp. $12.95 hardback.

Wyman, Donald
> Wyman's Gardening Encyclopedia. New York, Macmillan, 1971. 1222 pp. $17.50 hardback.

## GENERAL GARDENING BOOKS

Davis, Ben Arthur
> A Southern Garden. Philadelphia, J. B. Lippincott, 1971. 252 pp. $5.95 hardback.

Harshbarger, Gretchen Fischer
> McCall's Garden Book. New York, Simon & Schuster, 1967. 520 pp. $9.95 hardback.

Hastings, Donald & Louise
> The Southern Garden Book. Garden City, NY, Doubleday, 1948. 291 pp. $4.95 hardback.

Nuese, Josephine
> The Country Garden. New York, Charles Scribner's Sons, 1970. 256 pp. $2.95 paperback.

Pellegrini, Angelo M.
> The Food Lover's Garden. New York, Alfred Knopf, 1970. 253 pp. $6.95 hardback.

Rockwell, F. F. (Ed.)
> 10,000 Garden Questions. New York, Doubleday, 1944. 1390 pp. $8.95 hardback.

Stout, Ruth
> Gardening Without Work. Old Greenwich, CT, Devin-Adair, 1973. 214 pp. $4.95 hardback.

U.S.D.A.
> Growing Vegetables in the Home Garden: Home & Garden Bulletin #202. Washington, DC, 1972. G.P.O. 52 pp. 70¢ booklet.

Wiberg, Hugh
> Backyard Vegetable Gardening for the Beginner. New York, Exposition Press, 1971. 105 pp. $4.00 hardback.

Wickenden, Leonard
> Gardening With Nature. New York, Fawcett, 1972. 340 pp. 95¢ paperback.

## BERRIES, FRUITS & NUTS

Auf der Heide, Ralph
> The Illustrated Wine-Making Book. Garden City, NY, Doubleday, 1973. 206 pp. $2.95 paperback.

Hedrick, U. P.
> The Homestead Way to Grow Grapes. Charlotte, VT, Garden Way, 1945. Bulletin #10. 11 pp. 50¢

Kraft, Ken & Pat
> Fruits for the Home Garden. New York, William Morrow, 1968. 287 pp. $7.95 hardback.

Reed, Clarence Arthur
> The Improved Nut Trees of North America and How to Grow Them. New York, Devin-Adair, 1954. 404 pp. hardback.

Riotte, Louise
> Complete Guide to Growing Berries & Grapes. Charlotte, VT, Garden Way Publishing, 1974. 142 pp. $3.50 paperback.

Sibley, Celestine
> The Sweet Apple Gardening Book. Garden City, NY, Doubleday, 1972. 214 pp. $5.95 hardback.

Simmons, Alan E.
> Growing Unusual Fruit. New York, Walker & Co., 1972. 354 pp. $10.00 hardback.

Southwick, Lawrence
> Dwarf Fruit Trees for the Home Gardener. Charlotte, VT, Garden Way, 1972. 118 pp. $3.00 paperback.

Tritton, S. M.
> Amateur Wine-Making. New York, NY, Dover Publications, 1959. 241 pp. $5.00 hardback.

Wescheke, Carl
> Growing Nuts in the North. St. Paul, Webb Publishing, 1954. 124 pp. $2.00 hardback.

## Food Storage and Preparation

Blanchard, Marjorie P.
> Home Gardener's Cookbook. Charlotte, VT, Garden Way, 1974. 192 pp. $4.50 paperback.

Hertzberg, Vaughn & Greene
> Putting Food By. Brattleboro, VT, Stephen Greene Press, 1973. 364 pp. $6.95 hardback.

Levinson, Leonard
> The Complete Book of Pickles & Relishes. Charlotte, VT, Garden Way, 1965. 336 pp. $5.95 hardback.

Loveday, Evelyn
> The Complete Book of Home Storage of Vegetables & Fruits. Charlotte, VT, Garden Way, 1972. 148 pp. $3.00 paperback.

Macmaniman, Gen
> Dry It—You'll Like It. Fall City, WA, Living Foods Dehydrators, 1973. 58 pp. $3.95 paperback.

U.S.D.A.
> Home Canning of Fruits & Vegetables. Home & Garden Bulletin #8, Washington, DC, G.P.O., 1972. 32 pp. 20¢ booklet.

## SOIL

Bear, Firman E.
> Soils in Relation to Crop Growth. New York, Reinhold, 1965. 297 pp. $14.95 hardback.

Berger, Kermit C.
> Sun, Soil & Survival. Norman, OK, University of Oklahoma Press, 1972. 371 pp. $7.95 hardback.

Donahue, Roy L.; Shicklima, John C.; Robertson, Lynn S.
> Soils: An Introduction to Soils and Plant Growth. Englewood Cliffs, NJ, Prentice-Hall, 1971. 587 pp. hardback.

Hudson, Norman
> Soil Conservation. Ithaca, Cornell University Press, 1971. 320 pp. $9.75 hardback.

Ortloff, H. Stuart & Raymore, Henry B.
> A Book About Soils for the Home Gardener. New York, William Morrow, 1972. 189 pp. $2.45 paperback.

## SUPPLIES

Griffin Greenhouse Supplies, 1619 Main St., Tewksbury, MA 01876
Garden Way Research, Charlotte, VT 05445

## ENTOMOLOGY—PESTS AND DISEASES

Editors of Organic Gardening and Farming
> Getting the Bugs Out of Organic Gardening. Emmaus, PA, Rodale Press, 1973. 115 pp. $2.95 paperback.

Hunter, Beatrice Trum
> Gardening Without Poisons. Boston, Houghton Mifflin, 1971. 318 pp. $6.95 hardback.

Philbrick, John & Helen
    The Bug Book. Charlotte, VT, Garden Way, 1974. 144 pp. $3.50 paperback.
Swan, Lester A.
    Beneficial Insects. New York, Harper & Row, 1964. 429 pp. $7.95 hardback.

LIVESTOCK, POULTRY AND BEES

Bundy, Clarence E. & Diggins, Ronald V.
    Dairy Production. Englewood Cliffs, NJ, Prentice-Hall, 1954. 304 pp. $11.60 hardback.
Bundy, Clarence E. & Diggins, Ronald V.
    Livestock and Poultry Production. Englewood Cliffs, NJ, Prentice-Hall, 1968. 723 pp. $11.95 hardback.
Bundy, Clarence E. & Diggins, Ronald V.
    Swine Production. Englewood Cliffs, NJ, Prentice-Hall, 1956. 342 pp. $11.25 hardback.
Canada Dept. of Agriculture
    The Dairy Goat in Canada. Agri. Dept., Ottawa. 1971. Publication No. 1441.
Editors of Gleanings in Bee Culture
    Starting Right With Bees. Medina, OH, A. I. Root Company. 100 pp. $1.00 paperback.
Emery, Jim
    Backyard Dairy Book. New Park, PA (Box 4) 17352
Klein, G. T.
    Starting Right With Poultry. Charlotte, VT, Garden Way, 1947. 177 pp. $3.00 paperback.
Root, A. I.
    The ABC & XYZ of Bee Culture. Medina, OH, A. I. Root Co., 1966. 712 pp. $6.50 hardback.
Stamm, G. W.
    Veterinary Guide for Farmers. Charlotte, VT, Garden Way, 1963. 384 pp. $6.95 hardback.
Teller, Walter M.
    Starting Right With Sheep. Charlotte, VT, Garden Way, 1973. 60 pp. $1.50 paperback.
Templeton, George S.
    Domestic Rabbit Production. Danville, IL, The Interstate, 1968. 213 pp. $6.25 hardback.

Walsh, Helen
> Starting Right with Milk Goats. Charlotte, VT, Garden Way, 1947. 138 pp. $3.00 paperback.

## EQUIPMENT SOURCES

C. H. Dana Co., Hyde Park, VT 05655

Farnham Livestock Equipment Co., Box 2151, Phoenix, AZ 85001

United Pharmacal Co., 306 Cherokee St., St. Joseph, MO 64504 (veterinary supplies).

## HERBS & WILD FOODS

Atkins, F. C.
> Mushroom Growing Today. New York, Macmillan, 1967. 188 pp. $5.95 hardback.

Brooks, Joe
> Complete Guide to Fishing Across North America. New York, Outdoor Life—Harper & Row, 1966. 613 pp. $7.95 hardback.

Clarkson, Rosetta E.
> Herbs: Their Culture & Uses. New York, Macmillan, 1942. 226 pp. $5.95 hardback.

Edminster, Frank C.
> American Game Birds of Field and Forest. New York, Charles Scribner's Sons, 1954. 490 pp. $17.50 hardback.

Gibbons, Euell
> Stalking the Wild Asparagus. New York, McKay, 1962. 303 pp. $2.95 paperback.

Gibbons, Euell
> Stalking the Blue-Eyed Scallop. New York, McKay, 1964. 332 pp. $2.95 paperback.

Harris, Ben Charles
> Eat the Weeds. Barre, MA, Barre Publishers, 1961. 223 pp. $3.95 paperback.

Ormond, Clyde
> Complete Book of Hunting. New York, Outdoor Life—Harper & Row, 1962. 467 pp. $6.95 hardback.

Simmons, Adelma Grenier
> The Illustrated Herbal Handbook. New York, Hawthorn, 1964. 124 pp. $1.95 paperback.

Simmons, Adelma Grenier
> Herbs to Grow Indoors. New York, Hawthorn, 1969. 146 pp. $5.95
> hardback.

Smith, Alexander H.
> The Mushroom Hunter's Field Guide. Ann Arbor, University of Michigan Press, 1958. 264 pp. $9.95 hardback.

EQUIPMENT SOURCES

Herter's Inc. Mitchell, South Dakota 57301
L. L. Bean. Freeport, Maine 04032

SPECIAL TECHNIQUES

Campbell, Stu
> The Mulch Book. Charlotte, VT, Garden Way, 1973. 144 pp. $3.50
> paperback.

Editors of Organic Gardening & Farming
> Organic Fertilizers: Which Ones and How to Use Them. Emmaus, PA,
> Rodale Press, 1973. 123 pp. $2.95 paperback.

Editors of Organic Gardening & Farming
> 300 of the Most Asked Questions About Organic Gardening. Emmaus,
> PA, Rodale Press, 1972. 195 pp. $6.95 hardback.

Foster, Catherine Osgood
> The Organic Gardener. New York, Vintage, 1972. 234 pp. $2.95 paperback.

Goleuke, Clarence G.
> Composting: A Study of the Process and Its Principles. Emmaus, PA,
> Rodale Press, 1972. 110 pp. $2.95 paperback.

Heckel, Alice
> The Pfeiffer Garden Book—Biodynamics in the Home Garden. Stroudsburg, PA, Bio-Dynamic Farming & Gardening Association, 1967.
> 199 pp. $2.75 paperback.

Hunter, Beatrice Trum
> Gardening Without Poisons. Boston, Houghton Mifflin, 1971. 318 pp.
> $6.95 hardback.

Morse, Harriet K.
> Gardening in the Shade. New York, Charles Scribner's Sons, 1962.
> 242 pp. $2.95 paperback.

Northwest Companion Planter (periodical, $4 per year)
> 311 First Avenue South, Seattle, WA 98104

Philbrick, Helen & Gregg, Richard B.
> Companion Plants and How to Use Them. Old Greenwich, CT, Devin-Adair, 1966. 113 pp. $4.95 hardback.

## CONTAINER GARDENING & GREENHOUSING

Blake, Claire L.
> Greenhouse Gardening for Fun. New York, Morrow, 1967. 256 pp. $7.95 hardback; $2.45 paperback.

Flanagan, Ted
> Growing Food & Flowers in Containers. Charlotte, VT, Garden Way, 1974. 128 pp. $3.95 paperback.

Illinois Cooperative Extension Service
> Plastic Greenhouses. Urbana, IL, University of Illinois, 61801, 1965. Circular #705   25¢

Kramer, Jack
> Container Gardening Indoors & Out. Garden City, NY, Doubleday, 1971. 157 pp. $6.95 hardback.

McDonald, Elvin
> Gardening Under Lights. Garden City, NY, Doubleday, 1965. 213 pp. $5.95 hardback.

Truex, Philip
> City Gardener. New York, Alfred Knopf, 1964. $7.95 hardback.

## TOOLS

Food production will probably center around your garden. The following list of work and reading materials is by no means exhaustive, though we hope to have treated all the essential knowledge you will need. Tool prices are, again, approximate.

## GARDENING TOOLS—NON-POWERED

| | |
|---|---|
| fork | $ 5.00 |
| hoe | 3.00 |
| garden rake | 6.00 |
| spade | 5.75 |
| trowel | 2.00 |
| small hand rake | 2.00 |
| hand cultivator | 7.00 |
| wheel barrow or cart | 25–150.00 |
| spreader | 30–100.00 |

GARDENING TOOLS—POWERED

tiller, front end tines . . . . . . . . . . $300–400.00
tiller, rear end tines . . . . . . . . . . . 450–600.00
shredder . . . . . . . . . . . . . . . . 150.00
small tractor (with accessories) . . . . . . . 1,000 vicinity

# CHAPTER FIVE

# SYSTEMS: WATER, WASTE, HEAT, LIGHT

To be able to live on your land you must supply yourself with pure water, dispose of your waste, and heat and light your house. Your systems for performing these functions must be good ones. They not only must meet your needs over the years, but must meet the needs of the community and the land itself. These systems together may represent a greater investment than the building of your house, and they will certainly affect your homestead operation and happiness as much or more than any other factors. For these reasons, it is a good idea to consider the various methods and operations for providing *all* these services before you buy your land. You certainly should have them uppermost in mind as you inspect a possible homestead site.

## WATER

Good homesteading land must have an ample and unfailing supply of good water, especially good drinking water. As you look at your prospec-

tive land, check the presence of water (too much or too little) as well as its location. An ideal site will have a reliable spring, but if yours does not, it may have an existing well. As a last resort you may have to develop a new well.

## SPRINGS

If you have a spring, be sure it has an ample flow—four to six gallons a minute. Is it a year-round spring? Some springs dry up during July and August. Is it reasonably near your potential house site? If the answer to these questions is "yes," you probably have a reliable water supply. But have the water tested for purity and hardness, too.

Ideally, a spring should be located on high ground above the house; this will allow you to use a simple *gravity system*, as shown here. If water flows continuously from the spring, the pipe will not freeze. If the flow is not constant, bury the pipe below the frost line.

In many instances you will be lucky enough to have a spring, but unlucky that it is on low ground. If you must locate your house above the spring, you can pump the water uphill to a home storage tank. And if there is *some* downhill flow of water, you can pump with a *water ram,* which requires no electricity or other power but operates automatically. Water will stand in the pipes when not being drawn, so care must be taken in cold areas to bury them below the frost line, and also to protect the ram.

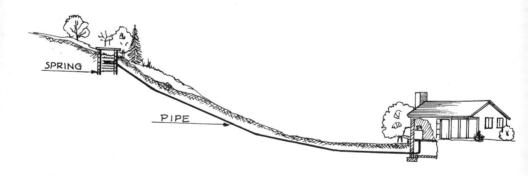

SPRING

PIPE

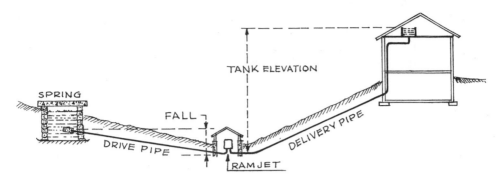

A third source of natural water is to tap into a stream or pond. However, unless you live in a very remote area, any surface water is likely to be polluted, especially a brook or stream. Check for up-stream neighbors and run a careful test on the water quality.

### EXISTING WELLS

Many farms and homesteads do not have a spring source of water, unfortunately. But many have wells, which are either hand-dug, drilled or driven.

*Dug wells* usually are seen on old farms that were in operation before electricity became common. They were dug with hand tools, and the sides were rocked or bricked up to prevent cave-ins. Despite rock walls, hand dug wells are more susceptible to groundwater contamination than are drilled wells. They also are likely to run dry when used with modern water pumps and modern plumbing, simply because these devices allow us to use (and often waste) much more water than our grandfathers did. Existing wells sometimes can be dug deeper to reach a greater flow of water, and a well that goes dry gives you a chance to take a close look at it and to clean it out. Properly built and cared for, a dug well can continue · to supply adequate pure water for generations to come.

It is still possible, of course, to dig wells by hand—a laborious undertaking, but one that may save you several hundred dollars. The basic trick is to dig a wide enough hole to keep it from caving in on you as you dig deeper. Some people even recommend digging in the winter, when the topsoil is frozen and much less likely to cave in. Start the hole in the fall

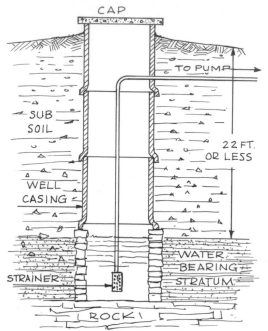

CAP

TO PUMP

SUB
SOIL

22 FT.
OR LESS

WELL
CASING

WATER
BEARING
STRATUM

STRAINER

ROCK!

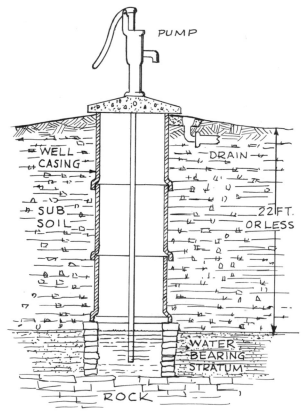

PUMP

WELL
CASING

DRAIN

SUB
SOIL

22 FT.
OR LESS

WATER
BEARING
STRATUM

ROCK

before the ground freezes and then continue it later in the winter. Of course, how far down you'll hit water—if at all—is never certain.

*Drilled wells* are more common today, primarily because of the availability of drilling equipment. They provide better protection against ground water seepage because they have casings that run down to water-bearing rock. You never know, though, how deep your drilled well may have to be. You may have to drill only 40 feet, which might cost $360 at $9 a foot. But if you have to drill 300 feet, you could spend $2,700 just for the drilling! Additional expenses include a pressure pump, a tank, pipe to the house and plumbing installation. Thus a drilled well is by far the most expensive water source—and it is impossible to determine in advance *how* expensive it will be. The only real clue you have is the depth of your neighbors' wells, which may indicate yours, if there is an even geological strata. In some areas deep well water is quite hard. However, a drilled well may be the best well or, under some circumstances, the only choice.

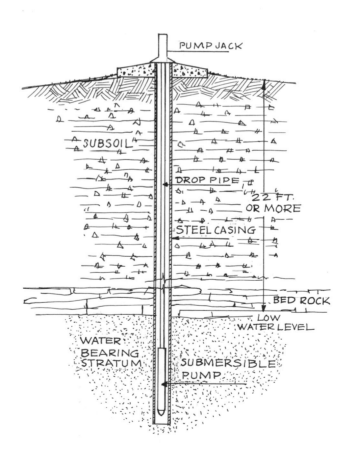

A third type is the _driven well,_ in which a pipe fitted with a well point is driven into water-bearing sand. This type of well is suitable only in special areas, but it costs much less than either a hand-dug or a drilled well.

## LOCATING WATER

Besides the mystery about the depth of a well, it is always somewhat uncertain where water is to be found. Many people have found that _dowsing_ is a useful and sometimes remarkably effective way to locate water and well-drilling locations. There are other methods, too—all of which have their supporters. A check around your local area will undoubtedly turn up a few professed "water witches" or dowsers.

## TOWN WATER

Many rural areas now have established water districts and have put in water lines to town or village residents. If you live close enough to the town water line, you may have a choice of whether to dig a well or tap into the town water. At first the well undoubtedly will cost more, depending on how deep you have to go. In the long run, however, the yearly cost of town water ($40-$100 a year) may make an individual well a better buy. If you are offered the choice, figure the cost over ten or twenty years before you decide that with town water your problems are magically solved. If fire hydrants come with the town water, figure that benefit in, too.

## WATER PURITY

Before you bought your land, you would have the spring, existing well or pond water tested by the local health department. This test would determine the presence of bacteria, physical or chemical pollution.

The most common source of bacteria in water is seepage from pasture areas or nearby septic tanks, sometimes caused by poorly-constructed wells or those which are too close to the tanks. In drilling a well, therefore, make certain that it is at least 50 feet from the nearest septic tank and 150 feet from any subsurface sewage disposal leach system. The best insurance against contamination is a properly cased well, an electric water pump, piped water and house taps. All these reduce possible contamination of the water to a minimum.

The physical characteristics of your water should not be objectionable. Turbidity, color and taste can vary from one area to another even if the water is safe. But if they are offensive, you may want to find another place for homesteading, or your local health department may have some suggestions for water treatment.

The *chemical* characteristics of your water may include fluorides, chlorides, sodium or nitrates. However, these chemicals usually are unnoticeable unless you are particularly sensitive.

One water quality you probably *will* notice is *hardness,* which is caused by dissolved calcium and magnesium salts. Water forms mineral deposits on the inside of water pipes and tanks; these deposits eventually can prevent the flow of water and make it necessary to install new pipes or tanks. On an everyday basis hardness is objectionable because it makes obtaining a soap or detergent lather difficult. Hardness can be reduced by using a zeolite water softener, though this is a costly process.

### WATER TREATMENT

Most towns maintain water treatment plants to insure pure water for residents, the most common process being the addition of chlorine. If you live in an area of poor water, such a treatment plant may help you decide to use town water.

Treatment may be too ambitious or expensive for your own water source, depending on your ability to adapt to tastes that may be safe but still somewhat unpalatable. Water treatment consists essentially of allowing particles to settle, filtering, and adding a disinfectant. All or none of these steps may be necessary. Check with your local county water authority or public health department for their advice.

### NON-DRINKING WATER

If well flow is insufficient or your well has not yet been dug, there are time-honored methods of gathering water for animals and for washing. One is the use or creation of a farm pond, usually the excavation of a low-lying, swampy area. Normal drainage will fill the pond to a consistent depth, and it can also be used for fishing and swimming.

RAIN WATER

Another method is catching rainwater from eavestroughs in barrels. Such water is perfectly good for watering animals and your garden in a dry spell or for washing clothes. Of course, any water you intend to use for drinking or cooking should be boiled.

Some homesteaders in low water areas provide for most or all of their water needs from rain water (which is naturally soft) by constructing home roof run-off systems which filter into very large storage cisterns in the basement.

WATER DISTRIBUTION

Early settlers hauled water in buckets from wells, springs and streams. Today we turn a faucet and get hot or cold water in a moment. But there are many possible steps in between that may be practicable for a rural homestead. The only general rule is that more sophisticated water systems cost more and usually provide better quality control of your water.

One easy improvement over a well with a hand pump is to have an overhead storage tank to which water is pumped by a water ram, hand or electric pump. From the storage tank water runs by gravity pressure to your taps. Such a tank can be placed in a freeze-proof attic, over a kitchen sink, or in an unused room. It would probably not provide the pressure needed for an automatic clothes washer, however. Another alternative is to have a gravity-fed cistern in the basement or under the kitchen counter, with a hand pump located at the kitchen sink—or an electric pump to provide tap pressure. Cistern storage may be useful, also, with a spring which is reliable but has a slow flow. Various arrangements are possible. Check with neighbors, or get advice on your personal system from a local contractor or plumber.

TROUBLE SPOTS

Besides well seepage, water quality and supply, the biggest problem of homestead water systems is likely to be frozen pipes. Outside pipes in

which the water stands (does not flow constantly) must be buried below the frost line, which will vary with your geographical area. Burying pipes is a back-breaking job if done by hand; in northern climates you may have to bury them four or more feet deep (in northern sections of Canada permafrost prevents normal pipeline use entirely).

Pipes most often freeze where they enter a basement or outside wall. To help prevent this, do not allow the pipe to rise close to the surface of the ground until it is within the warm radius of the building.

In houses with an established or recurring freezing problem, electric heat tape can be used to wrap the pipes. However, this is a stopgap measure rather than a permanent solution.

Remember that traffic drives frost deeper in the ground. Pipes under pathways and driveways, then, should be placed even deeper than your normal frost depth, perhaps 50 percent deeper to be safe.

## SEWAGE DISPOSAL

Closely related to a system for providing pure water for your homestead is your method of disposing of waste waters, particularly sewage. Whether you will have a waste problem depends largely on the permeability of your soil and the arrangement of your well, house and leach line system. As we mentioned in the chapter on buying land, the soil must have good drainage characteristics—slope, loose soil particles, a suitably low water table—for any sewage disposal method to work. The added water today's family uses also taxes disposal systems which were adequate in earlier times.

Assuming that the soil is satisfactory and likely to drain well, it still is important to keep your sewage system at a proper distance and direction from your water well, from nearby streams, and from your farm pond where animals may drink. The illustrations following show the necessary distance between well and cesspool or septic tank.

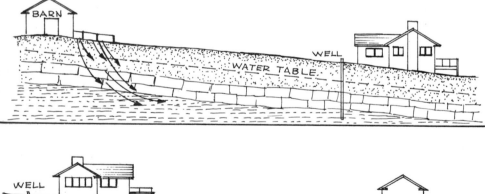

As we have shown, the well should be located near the house. If there is a slope, the spring or well might be above the house and the waste system below both well and house.

In addition, a privy, cesspool or septic system must not drain either into the water table or into surface water. Sewage should be leached through a middle stratum of earth.

SEPTIC SYSTEMS

Septic systems are the most common and preferred waste disposal method for individual households because they can be used with running water and flush toilets. A septic system has two parts: the *septic tank,* which allows solids to settle out and decompose bacterially, and the *leaching fields,* through which effluent water is absorbed into the soil. Following is shown the basic construction of a septic tank and leach fields.

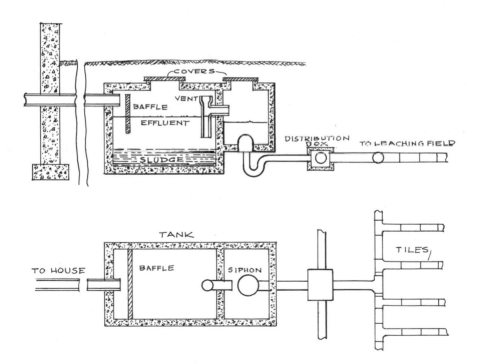

Besides their initial cost, the main objection to septic tank systems is the heavy work of repairs when the system breaks down.

One important way to keep a septic system free of trouble is to be careful about what goes *into* the system. Too much soap, grease and detergent can halt the bacterial action in the tank. Septic tanks also work better in warm weather and are most likely to have problems in winter. Passing hot water through the system can be helpful in preventing cold weather clogging. Sometimes yeast and special preparations flushed down to the tank will revive the tank's action. At best the tank probably will have to be pumped out every few years.

There are special tables to figure the proper septic tank size and length of leaching lines for various conditions of use. The more fluids that go into a tank, the more leach field is needed. But no septic tank can maintain its bacterial action if excessive amounts of water are put into it. Try to send your laundry water into another leach system or a dry well. The cost, varying according to the size of the system you need and the amount of work you are willing to do yourself, probably will average $400–$500. For more information on septic systems, see the chapter index.

There are other sewage systems, of course, the most basic being the ordinary outhouse or pit privy, as described below. The other methods mentioned here are largely desired for special circumstances—either water shortages, frozen ground (permafrost), or for the homesteader determined to use a waste system that recycles some of the waste products.

PIT PRIVIES

In times past and in many places today the *pit privy* has been the old standby for sewage disposal. Although it is one of the safest methods of waste disposal, the privy has the esthetic disadvantages of being slightly smelly and inconvenient. Note also that in some areas privies are not legal. A privy should be located on high ground, so that surface water will not flow through the pit. If no high ground is available, the privy can be built on its own mound of heaped earth. Be sure to keep it clean and well ventilated. Give it a coat of paint inside and out, use screened windows and keep the door and seat closed when not in use. More elaborate suggestions might include a fiberglass roof for daylight or an electric light. Cut down odor by sprinkling lye or wood ashes into the pit after each use.

SAVING WATER

One problem with modern flush toilets is that they use about five gallons of water each time they flush—more than is needed. You can cut down on this amount by placing bricks or rocks in your toilet tank to displace some of the water, or by bending the float arm so the tank doesn't fill completely.

Various kinds of toilets are available that do not use so much water as the flush type. Some, in fact, use none at all. These include the *bucket toilet, chemical toilet* (often used on planes and boats), the *minimum-flush-water toilet* and the *incinerating toilet*. Most are expensive and inconvenient to operate, but each is useful under special conditions where the cycle must be self-contained or where water is particularly scarce.

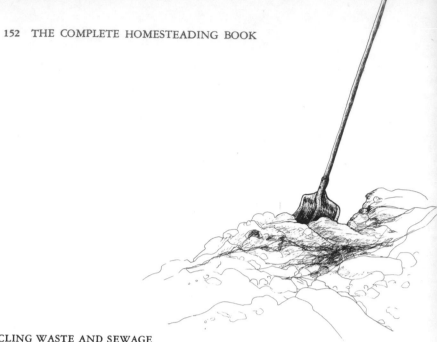

## RECYCLING WASTE AND SEWAGE

Some homesteaders have carried the recycling concept to its logical conclusion by recycling their own waste. One way to do so, but which is illegal in most areas, is spreading composted human manure on the land —that is, composting the privy waste. A more efficient and acceptable ap-

proach is the *compost privy,* which converts all animal and human waste into two products: fertilizer and methane gas. The fertilizer can then be used on the garden and the methane gas used to run converted automobiles or cooking stoves. One intriguing move in this direction is the *Clivus* toilet, which is almost unknown in the United States. Information about such toilets and sewage recycling is available through *The Mother Earth News* (see Chapter Seven appendix).

# HEATING

As a homesteader you probably are not interested in the expensive and conventional central heating systems used in most houses. Central heating, of course, involves a furnace and heat ducts or pipes that carry the heat evenly throughout an entire house. If you are, see any one of the many available books on standard home heating. *Electric heat* is cheaper to install and allows individual room control. But electric power today is scarce and costly when used in this way. Rather than have an electric or central heating system most homesteaders heat with wood stoves or use a combination of wood, oil, gas, or even solar heat.

WOOD

In most rural areas, with the exception of the Plains states, Southwest and the Far West (where hardwoods are scarce), wood is a cheap method of heating. If you own a woodlot, you can procure your fuel supply for the winter at very little cost in two weeks or so of felling, cutting, hauling and splitting wood. Naturally this means using axes and saws, perhaps a horse or tractor, and often some neighborly help—but none of these is a very expensive investment. In *Living the Good Life,* Scott Nearing estimated that his house required four cords of fuel wood in a year and he could cut a cord of wood a day.

The most important things in heating with wood are that the wood be *hardwood* and that it be *seasoned.* Seasoned wood, which has been split and allowed to dry for at least six months, will burn much better and hotter than green wood, and you won't need so much of it.

In buying or cutting firewood, therefore, it is important to know and recognize not only seasoned wood, but the hardwoods that will give you the most heat. The most desirable common woods are beech, white ash, oak, hickory, yellow birch and maple as well as the fruit woods. For more information, see the chapter appendix.

In *Organic Gardening,* March, 1973, Jeff Cox gives a useful formula for determining the number of cords of wood you will need to heat your house for a winter. He takes into consideration the size of house, quality of insulation and climate to arrive at the number of BTU's required. He then compares this figure with the BTU's produced by a cord of various kinds of wood. He concludes that an average farm house in the North may require eight or nine cords of seasoned hardwood.

One last note: Wood should be stored under cover in a well-ventilated wood shed, back room or section of your barn. It should not be left exposed to rain and snow, but it may be seasoned stacked outside if the top is covered. As Scott Nearing points out dry wood under cover is your money in the bank.

### FRANKLIN AND THERMOSTATIC STOVES

For heating a home or other homestead building, there are two basic kinds of wood stoves: those that simply burn wood, and those that use a thermostatically adjusted draft and airtight firebox, sometimes with a blower attachment, to control the burning. The second type, needless to say, is more efficient and consumes less wood. The Franklin and other simple wood-burning stoves represent a considerable advance over fireplaces for efficient heating. However, the thermostatic stoves represent an equally great advance over the Franklin.

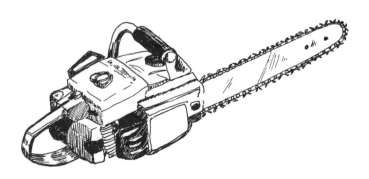

The best-known examples of thermostatic wood burners are Ashley and Riteway. Both come in various sizes and styles. People who use Ashleys invariably are enthusiastic about them, especially their reduction of the necessary woodpile (from nine to perhaps four or five cords), and their ability to burn up to twelve hours without stoking. They thus reduce two of the most onerous aspects of wood heating—keeping the woodbox full and constantly tending the fire.

As a general rule if you really want to heat with wood, you're definitely better off buying one or two of these stoves. It is a substantial expense, but in the end you'll save money. (See chapter appendix for manufacturers' addresses.)

During the recent great demand for wood stoves, many companies have begun to market simple sheet metal or welded steel wood stoves. Some are well designed and built, but some are flimsy, inefficient and even unsafe. Look them over carefully.

It's worth making a distinction between thermostatic draft stoves and the old cast iron kitchen wood ranges that people have used for cooking and heating for many years. Many people still use and love them, but nobody likes their excessive heat in summer. To make summer cooking something less than torture, most homesteaders abandon wood fuel and use a gas range for warm-weather cooking. Some kitchen stoves are available that convert from wood to gas or oil for just this situation, or some will use both fuels.

All stoves must be carefully and safely installed and maintained. Pay particular attention to a fireproof base pad, adequate distance from flammable walls, sound stove pipes and pipe fitting, and the condition of your chimney. These precautions are outlined in more detail later, under Miscellaneous Homestead Systems.

FIREPLACES

No country home really is complete without a fireplace. It adds warmth, friendliness and a sense of security to the smallest cabin. Besides providing enjoyment, a fireplace adds greatly to the appearance and value of any house.

However, the fireplace without doubt is the most inefficient heating device there is. First, about 80 percent of the heat goes up the chimney rather than into the room. Second, the fire sucks a draft of air that may actually cool parts of the room, as outside air is drawn in through cracks and crevices.

The solution is not to abandon the idea of a fireplace. Rather, abandon the idea that your fireplace will heat your house or any substantial part of it. Simply enjoy it for its cheer. And if you can, arrange a fire draft from behind or below that will not drain cool air from the rest of the room.

One practical way to give a fireplace the air it needs is to install a grill or register in the floor in front of the hearth or behind the fire box, connected to the cellar or outside. This will keep your updraft in one place and will reduce the amount of already-heated air that goes up the chimney. An adjustable damper helps, too.

The efficiency of a fireplace also can be increased by building it open on three sides and using a hood overhead. Another improvement for standard fireplaces provides heat boxes beside the fireplace to convert warm air into the room. This system depends on the installation of cast iron or copper-surfaced heat ducts in the masonry; they must be installed at the time your fireplace is being built.

*Construction.* The construction of fireplaces is a definite art, and many books have been written describing fireplace fashions and building tech-

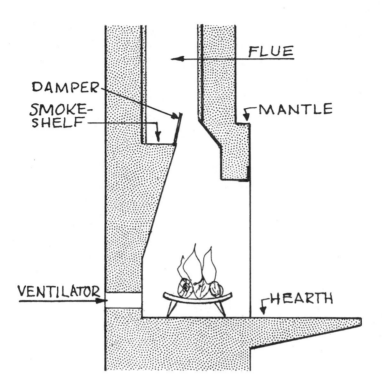

niques (see chapter appendix). Without going into elaborate detail, here are the basic fireplace features.

The *damper* prevents heat loss up the chimney when the fireplace is not in use and sometimes can adjust the draft. The *slanted back* of the fireplace reflects heat into the room and aims the smoke at the smoke shelf. The *ventilator* provides the air that the fire needs, as mentioned above. Various mistakes can be made in construction, or the chimney later can become clogged. For more information about building and enjoying fireplaces, see *The Fireplace Book* by Vrest Orton and "Curing Smoky Fireplaces" by Garden Way Publishing. For a discussion of unusual fireplace design, see *The Owner-Built Home* by Ken Kern.

OIL BURNERS

Oil-burning or kerosene stoves also are available, some which stand in the room and heat by radiance; others which stand in a basement like a central heating furnace. The drawbacks to unvented oil stoves is that they can be dangerous and usually have a noticeable smell. They also consume fuel oil, which must not only be paid for in cash, but is becoming scarcer and costlier as world oil reserves are depleted. Fuel oil must be delivered, which also can be a problem in remote areas.

The only advantages to oil-burning stoves I can think of are the saving of labor in cutting wood and the freedom from having to stoke the heater. In all other respects it is much less desirable than the wood burner.

*Gas stoves.* Gas, such as propane or butane, also can be a useful source of homestead heat. It shares with oil many disadvantages, such as cost, delivery problems, malfunctioning dangers, short supply and lack of innate attractiveness. However, it is probably cleaner and in some areas may be cheaper to buy.

Gas cooking stoves are quite useful and can be a good alternative to wood for warm weather cooking. They are certainly preferable to electric ranges, which consume huge amounts of power and produce high electric bills. Gas ranges also are invulnerable to power failures or blackouts, giving one at least a small measure of independence.

SOLAR HEAT

"Solar heat" is a term that has many meanings, depending on whom you're reading or listening to. It usually is meant for enlightened home-builders as an advanced, cheap, and ecologically sound method of heating, but precisely *what* it means can be confusing. It can mean anything from an elaborate heat-retaining and distributing system to the use of sunlight to reduce standard heating bills.

The simplest form of solar heating that I have encountered is in Rex Roberts' *Your Engineered House.* This is the siting and building of a home to take maximum advantage of the sun. This sort of solar heating involves pointing the house in the right direction, placing walls, primarily of glass, on the south side and constructing the house so that nearly every room has a southern exposure.

In this sense solar heat is an excellent way to reduce your artificial heating bill—possibly, if your winters are sunny and the house is well insulated, by as much as half. Other configurations are possible, of course, but the idea remains the same—to let the sun do the heating it is capable of in the winter. If the angles and materials and house layout are properly chosen, Roberts points out, this kind of supplementary heating can be an important factor.

Other types of solar heating go forward from here. Because sunny days may be rare in winter, and because the nights are especially cold, some method must be found to *retain* the sun's heat—to store it up. Among the many methods, one proposed by Dr. Marie Telkes uses five-gallon cans of salts in a special heat storage chamber, situated within a circle of naturally flowing air. Important to many heat-retaining proposals is the use of interior gardens, black matte walls for maximum heat absorption and dead air spaces with reflecting interior surfaces. The problems of solar heating are extremely complex, and already have inspired several books and unusual experiments. This undoubtedly will prove to be an important area of new developments for homesteaders in the near future. For additional information and source readings, see the chapter index.

*Other factors in heating systems.* Besides your source of heat there are many other considerations in cutting your heating costs. Insulation, prevailing winds, degree day totals, sunny days per year, terrain, building materials, and use of double doors and windows, all will affect your heating bills and comfort. Many of these already have been discussed in the chapter on building and planning the homestead and are mentioned here only briefly.

*Insulation.* To be heated efficiently your house must be well-insulated, preferably with fiberglass or polyurethane foam. But good, too, and much cheaper is *dead air space,* which can be built into the walls and roof during construction. The most important area to insulate is the attic or roof, since warm air seeks to escape upward. As I mentioned, careful construction of double doors (entryways) and double or storm windows will help greatly to retain house heat. For older country houses, closing off unneeded rooms in winter as a buffer between outside and heated living area also is a good idea.

*Prevailing winds.* Protection from north winds and storms always is desirable. Besides building below a hilltop or on the south side of a hill, a windscreen of evergreens or outbuildings will help to cut your heat losses (as well as snow drifting problems). The *terrain* is always a related consideration. Sometimes you can find a house site that is naturally sheltered from snow and wind but open to the sun in winter. In summer, too, some shade trees can cut your heat accumulation drastically and keep your house naturally cool.

*Building materials.* Most building materials will expand and contract as temperatures change. Green lumber in particular will shrink during the years after it is cut. If it is used in your house, you may find nails pulling loose and spaces opening above walls and in floors. Wooden doors, ironically, tend to expand and stick during warm wet weather when a little accidental draft would be welcome; they shrink during the dryness of winter, allowing the cold air to enter. But there are solutions for these problems and others: materials ranging from suburban aluminum siding (no maintenance) to spray-on foam (as discussed in Chapter Three) to different sorts of door construction (see Roberts's *Your Engineered House*).

In cold climates it often is a good idea to "bank" a house during winter—that is, to use piled hay or plastic sheeting to protect the foundation and sills from cold winds. The books listed in the chapter appendix, and your neighbors, will be able to give you many more important tips for retaining the heat on raw winter days.


## LIGHT AND POWER

One of the most exciting areas of homestead experimenting today is the home generation of electric power—part of the continuing effort to make individual homesteads truly self-sufficient. Because of the widespread use and value of freezers, basic electric machinery and home appliances, most homesteaders are not content to live without electricity, which, after all, is clean, relatively cheap and silent. (Older methods of lighting will be of interest to a minority as a permanent home system, but they will be discussed at the end of this section.

It is possible to generate your own electric power. The problem is to do

it more cheaply, to store it and have enough, compared to what you can buy from a power company. The basic methods involve using wind, water, gasoline engines, methane gas engines or perhaps the sun.

*Wind generators.* Wind generation has become one of the most popular bases for homestead power, especially as developed by Henry Clews (see chapter appendix). Clews has written a booklet describing the basic considerations in wind generation: size of wind blades, angles, your choice of wind speed for maximum generation and electric storage. Naturally the installation of a wind generator can be expensive—more than you would pay for several years' electric power. But in the long run it might be worthwhile, particularly if electric service is not nearby. Wind generation, of course, is more suitable in some areas than others—probably ideal for the Plains states—for it depends mostly on relatively steady (rather than gusty) wind patterns. Power storage and output are the main deterrents.

*Gasoline and methane engine generators.* Everybody is familiar with the problems of noise and pollution associated with gasoline engines, and the fuel supply problems today. Probably gasoline generators are best reserved for emergency situations as a backup source of power. Methane generators represent an important improvement, but still involve noise and the use of machinery (for compression of the gas) that can fail. Methane generation probably can be cheaper than wind generation, although not enough has been done with it to provide conclusive information. *The Mother Earth News* is one of the best sources of information on methane and other generating systems, but there are other sources (see chapter appendix).

*Water power* of course is used by gigantic hydroelectric plants to generate electricity, but whether it is suitable for individual installations is another question. My own guess is that water power generation is more expensive and difficult to set up than wind generation. Perhaps it would be preferable under some circumstances if a stream site is available. If you are really interested, follow up the listings in the chapter appendix.

Any sort of homestead power generation, of course, will represent an important investment, it is impossible to say how much since methods are changing constantly. Probably most homesteaders will choose to use the electricity supplied by power companies, which costs only a few dollars a month, for light and small appliances. Some people, however, located in remote areas, where the cost of bringing in power lines is prohibitive,

really have no choice but to generate their own power if they want electricity. Otherwise they must look to older methods of lighting their homes and preserving their food (see Chapter Four on traditional food storage). Note, however, that freezers and refrigerators are available which operate on gas rather than electricity. The other choices are kerosene and gasoline lamps and lanterns, and candles.

*Kerosene lamps.* One alternative—and a good one—to electric lighting is the Aladdin kerosene lamp, which produces 100 watts of steady white light. Such lamps cost $35 to $50 apiece, but they are much cleaner and more efficient than old-fashioned kerosene lanterns. Unlike pressure lamps, they also are quiet and can burn up to 50 hours on a single gallon of fuel. At this writing, however, kerosene was getting scarce, too, and expensive.

*Gasoline lanterns* are manufactured primarily for camp use, and they provide a very bright white light on unleaded gasoline. Their disadvantage is the noise of gas being released and burned under pressure. In addition the

mantles are very fragile, and gasoline can be a dangerous product for everyday table use. These lanterns are considerably cheaper than Aladdin lamps. White gas is relatively expensive and special fuel is especially so.

*Lanterns and candles.* For home lighting ordinary candles or kerosene lanterns provide the worst (but cheapest) sort of light. Though candles certainly can be charming, they are probably unsuitable for everyday use. Kerosene lanterns can be bought for three or four dollars, and candles, of course, can be made at home (see chapter appendix).

## MISCELLANEOUS HOMESTEAD SYSTEMS

*Lightning protection.* In some locations homesteaders will want to install lightning rods for house and barn protection. The advisability of doing so can be determined by a check with the neighbors, and such a precaution may prove to be worthwhile, though a professional installation is costly. Check your state fire marshal's office for approved companies.

*Fire protection.* You definitely will want to work out a fire protection system to safeguard the home you have spent much thought and energy creating. The obvious place to start is by building logical precautions into your heating and lighting systems. Be sure your chimney and fireplace are properly built, ventilated and maintained; install electric wiring properly and follow recommended safe practices; allow enough space around wood stove boxes and stove pipes. Use asbestos sheeting where it passes through a house wall. Keep the area around the stove clear, and install a brick or other fireproof pad to catch any falling embers and shield the floor from fire.

Besides these measures, clean chimney flues once or twice each year, keep freeze-proof fire extinguishers around, and make sure everybody knows where they are. Install stand-by hoses that will allow you to pump well or pond water to a possible shed or house fire. If you have an attic water tank, you can devise a valve to divert it quickly into a fire-fighting hose.

All of these ideas are little more than common sense—simply putting your existing systems to double use and planning exactly what means you will have at hand if a fire occurs. A farm pond, too, can be a house saver even if the nearest fire department is some miles away.

*Snow removal.* In the snow belt similar measures and precautions should be taken for snow removal. Ordinary snow accumulation is not a serious problem, but a storm at the wrong time (during an emergency) suddenly can create serious trouble. In the Midwest and western states blizzards can quickly obscure landmarks, keep animals unfed for days and thwart all attempts to reach outside help.

Ordinary snow precautions include avoiding a long driveway that must be plowed, or constructing a circular driveway (see Chapter Three) that can be used easily by the town snowplow. In building your house, give some thought to snowdrift patterns or plan to use snow fences. The same windbreaks that keep your house warm also can stop drifting snow and actually create a snowdrift barrier, saving you hours of shoveling or plowing. In areas where vehicles have a hard time in winter you might have reason to consider a four-wheel-drive truck.

*Transportation.* Keeping vehicles in good repair is important, especially to avoid frequent and costly visits to the local garage mechanic. Besides your garage and warm work space suggested in Chapter Four, you will need a good set of tools for car, truck or tractor repair, together with stocked supplies of plugs, filters, oils, grease and gasoline. For occasional help with heavy jobs a rigged block and tackle is almost essential. See chapter appendix for auto and truck repair manuals.

## SUMMARY

Before deciding where to build, what to build or even what land to buy, give careful thought to the various systems that you will need and the specific requirements of your homestead. An immense amount of information is available, especially from university extension services, public health offices, as well as product manufacturers and local agricultural agents. Taking time to think your home systems through beforehand will save you hundreds or thousands of dollars, both during construction and years later.

Heating systems, for example, are fairly simple once you get away from central installations. You will have to balance your time and energy against the available cash and your own preferences. Plumbing, too, is an area in which to save money and later maintenance. Ken Kern's *Owner-Built Home* can give you many imaginative ideas here. Doing without electric power causes many complications, and most homesteaders choose to use some electricity because of the freedom it gives to employ power tools and in lighting. At the same time it is perfectly possible to live happily without it, as Helen and Scott Nearing did for many years. Perhaps using no electricity will make life simpler and more agreeable for you, too.

Whatever your final choices, investigate your basic systems carefully before going ahead. Like buying land, the investment of time and thought at the very beginning is terribly important.

# APPENDIX

## SUGGESTED READING AND EQUIPMENT SOURCES

HEATING

*Books*

Conklin, Groff
> The Weather Conditioned House. New York, Reinhold Publishing Company, 1958.

Daniels, George
> Home Guide to Plumbing, Heating & Air Conditioning. New York, Harper & Row, 1967. 186 pp. $2.50 paperback.

Emerick, Robert
> Heating Handbook. New York, McGraw-Hill Company, 1964. $17.50 hardback.

Havens, David
> The Wood-Burners' Handbook. Box 1776, Portland, ME. Media House, 1974. $2.50 paperback.

U.S.D.A.
> An Economical and Efficient Heating System for Homes. (Production research report #99). Washington, U.S.D.A., 1967. 26 pp. 20¢ pamphlet.

U.S.D.A.
> Peripheral Circulation for Low-Cost Central Heating in Old Houses. (Production research report #124). Washington, U.S.D.A., 1971. 14 pp. 15¢ pamphlet.

*Equipment Sources*

> Ashley Automatic Heater Co., Box 730, Sheffield, AL 35660
> Portland Store Foundry Co., 57 Kennebec St., Portland, ME 04109
> Riteway Manufacturing Company, Box 6, Harrisonburg, VA 22801

## PLUMBING

Day, Richard
> Practical Handbook of Plumbing & Heating, New York, Arco Publishing.

## WATER, WASTE DISPOSAL

*Books*

Chambers, Howard V.
> Dowsing, Water Witches, Divining Rods. Los Angeles, CA, Sherbourne Press, 1969. $2.50 paperback.

Fair, Gordon Maskew & Geyer, John Charles
> Elements of Water Supply and Waste Water Disposal. New York, Wiley, 1965. 615 pp. $17.95 hardback.

Imhoff, Karl; Muller, W. J.; & Thistlethwayte, D. K. B.
> Disposal of Sewage and Other Water-borne Wastes. Ann Arbor, Ann Arbor Science Publisher, 1971. 405 pp. $16.80 hardback.

Linsley, Ray K. & Franzini, Joseph B.
> Water-Resources Engineering. New York, McGraw-Hill, 1964. 690 pp. $18.50 hardback.

Manual of Individual Water Supply Systems
> Department of HEW
> Superintendent of Documents
> United States Government Printing Office
> Washington, D.C. 20402
> 60¢ pamphlet

Rural Water Supplies. Circular #145, Vermont Extension Service, University of Vermont, Burlington, VT 05401

Sanitation Manual for Isolated Regions. Health & Welfare Dept., Ottawa, Canada (free)

Wagner, E. G.

> Excreta Disposal for Rural Areas and Small Communities. 1958, American Public Health Association, 1740 Broadway, NY, NY 10019, $5.00.
>
> Water Supply for Rural Areas and Small Communities. 1959 (see above for address).

Zimmerman, Josef D.

> Irrigation. New York, John Wiley & Sons, 1966. 516 pp. $6.75 hardback.

## Equipment Sources

> Deeprock Manufacturing Co., Box 870, Opelika, AL 36801
> Dempster Industries, Inc., P.O. Box 848, Beatrice, NE 68310
> Rife Hydraulic Engine Manufacturing Co., Box 367, Millburn, NJ 07041

## WIND POWER

### Books

Clews, Henry

> Electric Power from the Wind. Charlotte, VT, Garden Way, 1973. 29 pp. $2.00 booklet.

### Equipment Sources

> Bucknell Engineering Co., 10717 E. Rush St., S. El Monte, CA
> Dempster Industries, Inc., P.O. Box 848, Beatrice, NE 68310
> Solar Wind Co., RD 2, E. Holden, ME 04429

## HYDRO-ELECTRIC

### Equipment Sources

> James Leffel and Company, Springfield, OH 45501

## SOLAR HEAT

Halacy, D. S., Jr.

> The Coming Age of Solar Energy. New York, Harper & Row, 1973. 231 pp. $7.95 hardback.

### METHANE

New Alchemy Institute
> Methane Digesters for Fuel, Gas & Fertilizer. Woods Hole, MA, 1973. 47 pp. $3.00 pamphlet.

*Equipment Sources*

> Earth More, P.O. Box 13036, Washington, D.C. 20009
> Harold Bate, Pennyrowder, Blackawton, Totnes-Devon, TQ 97 Dr, England.

### LIGHTING

*Equipment Sources*

> Aladdin Industries, Kerosene Lamp Division, Nashville, TN 37210
> Eagle Kerosene Lamps, Thermwell Products Co., 152 E. 7th St., Paterson, NJ 07524

### AUTOMOTIVE

Ozy, Richard
> How to Service & Repair Your Own Car. New York, Arco Publishing, 1973. $10.95 hardback.

Forier, S. A. E. (Ed.)
> Motor's Auto Repair Manual, 1974. New York, Hearst Corporation, 1973. 1224 pp. $10.95 hardback.

Forier, S. A. E. (Ed.)
> Motor's Truck and Diesel Repair Manual. New York, Hearst Corporation, 1973. 1320 pp. $17.00 hardback.

CHAPTER SIX

# THE ECONOMICS OF HOMESTEADING

Homesteading differs from city life in two major ways, which become more pronounced as one's homestead becomes more established and successful. One is the replacement of a *direct* cash consumption system by a *direct* "productive homestead" system. The second difference is the gradual centering of one's work on the homestead instead of on an outside job. These differences are essential to homestead economics.

### INDIRECT VS. DIRECT CONSUMPTION

Most people who live and work in the city supply their needs indirectly; that is, they work for cash and exchange the cash for various store-bought goods, for food, cars, tools and housing. The homesteader, on the contrary, tries to limit his consumption of store-bought products by substituting homegrown and homemade food, shelter and entertainment. He tries to reduce his dependence on outside products as far as he comfortably can.

In the country, for example, one works directly on building a house, growing a garden, feeding the ducks and cutting fuel wood. The work eventually will become or produce the food and shelter you need. You are obtaining your needs directly, and for the most part paying not with cash but with your time, energy and skills.

The practical effect of this change to a direct home economy is a steadily decreased need for cash expenditures, a decreased dependence on outside full-time work, and a more satisfying and creative existence. What it does require, though, is initial capital to get it started.

## OUTSIDE AND HOMESTEAD WORK

Because of the tremendous amount of physical work and time involved in homesteading—building barns, haying, cutting wood, feeding and milking animals—it is almost impossible to keep a full-time job and still be a homesteader as we define the term. It becomes necessary to free yourself from most outside work simply to have the time that your homestead requires.

This distinction between outside and homestead work is possibly its basic difference from suburban living, where one can, after all, have a garden or even keep a few rabbits. Imagine a newspaper editor "freeing" himself from his job in the afternoons in order to have time to tidy up his apartment. The idea is ridiculous, because in the city his food, shelter and other comforts all depend on his employment income. He has to have cash to have anything else.

Despite the reduced need for cash on a homestead, some regular need for new money *does* remain, as well as the very important need for initial capital. This, then is the problem of homesteading economics: how to gather the initial capital, and how to reconcile the need for work both on and off the homestead.

# CASH NEEDS

## CAPITAL

The basic cash need in homesteading is *capital* to use as a down payment or outright payment for land, a house and additional beginning expenses—and these can be staggering. Even a minimal estimate of initial expenses will run into thousands of dollars when land must be paid for at present prices and a safety margin allowed for perhaps a year of homestead living without much income. For this reason, accumulating capital is the first (and most difficult) requirement for the would-be homesteader.

The most common way to put together the necessary capital, unfortunately, is to work full time for years and save. This is both difficult and frustrating, but such a long-term savings program is much easier when one has a definite goal in mind. Each month of work then brings one closer to the anticipated move.

Sometimes the most satisfactory course is to make a move from a city to a country *job*, especially in the area where one would like eventually to be homesteading. Such a move can be invaluable in really getting to know a rural area without cutting off one's source of regular income. Another good arrangement, if distances aren't great, is to keep a city job and work on a country place on weekends. Whatever your choice, the transition to a homestead is likely to be rough when you are still trying to meet heavy payments. Remember that many homesteaders had considerable savings before they decided to move to the country. Those who did not faced a doubly difficult situation.

The LORD Jesus (Jehovah) has provided (inch)

ESTIMATING CAPITAL NEEDS

In Chapter Two we estimated initial cash needs at about $5,000 bare minimum. This is probably a good figure to keep in mind, but there are so many variables that you definitely should tabulate your own prospective finances in detail. If you have savings, if you can get favorable loans, if your family can provide some help, you may be able to start with less.

Here are some major items to consider as you plan your future homestead:

*Land.* Land prices are rising everywhere. Plan to spend at least $1,000 an acre, especially if you are looking for less than ten acres. If this is too much, you may be able to do better if you are persistent and avoid popular places. Remember, too, that mortgages are easier to get if the land already has an existing house on it.

*House.* House costs vary wildly, and you may decide to save money by building a home yourself. Check costs with a builder, if you have a specific kind of house in mind, or allow a total sum that you are determined to

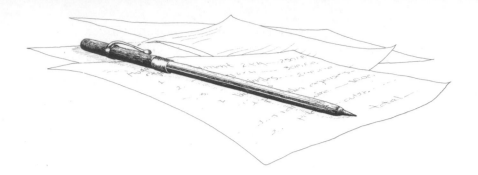

stay within. Some people, of course, have built perfectly livable houses for as low as $2,000, but to do so, they had to do all the labor themselves and really scrounge for materials.

*Vehicle*. Is your present vehicle suitable for the terrain and uses of the homestead? If not, you will need to add the cost of another or a different vehicle. In any case plan on higher repair bills for a year ahead.

*Animals*. If you plan to have animals right away, what will their expenses be? Include their purchase, the food, barns, fencing and probably vet bills. Remember that you are not likely to make a profit on your animal enterprises the first year.

*Improvements*. Almost certainly you will find some improvements and renovations are necessary, particularly if you move into an old farmhouse and use old buildings. Despite your efforts to keep such expenses to a minimum, they may run 10 to 15 percent of your purchase cost and should be figured in the initial cost total.

*Tools and other supplies*. Saws, axes, nails, screws, glass, oil and all sorts of other items will add up. Don't overlook them in figuring your starting expenses.

*Miscellaneous costs*. Even if you figure your initial costs carefully, unforeseen miscellaneous expenses are likely—such as for surveying, water testing, land sale closing, woodlot lumber estimates, special tools, house repairs and medical expenses. Be sure to include a safety margin of capital for these unexpected things. How large a safety margin is hard to say, but an additional 20 percent above your maximum figures probably is wise.

What you will have after all this calculating is a rough estimate of your initial homesteading costs, both outright payments and general expenses for the first few months. Those who wish to be especially careful might well include all living expenses for the first year, since the transition period is apt to be one of undependable income.

## MAKING THE TRANSITION

I think it is wise to ease slowly into a new life, especially something like homesteading, which is so dependent on personal skills, determination, stamina and a certain amount of luck. One is bound to make mistakes at first—mistakes that are likely to be paid for in cash and wasted time. Even if everything goes well, it takes several years to have a homestead running efficiently.

One of the major points of agreement among the homesteaders I have talked to is precisely this: *the dangerous tendency for beginners to try to do too much right at first.* It is simply too much to leave a job, move, buy land, build a house, start a garden and raise chickens and earn money —all in a few months. Burning your bridges is exciting—but at the right time. Plan your move to a homestead carefully and try to arrange both capital and a dependable source of income for the first few years. As we shall see, the best transition is often a gradual one.

## ROUTINE CASH NEEDS

Many homesteaders like to think that once they have bought their land and built a house, their need for cash somehow will disappear. This is only partly true, for no matter how self-sufficient you hope to be, you will always need a fairly regular cash income to meet routine expenses. These expenses will vary from small items like nails, shoelaces and paring knives to larger needs like a snowplow, work horse, henhouse or a new roof.

One method of figuring your routine living costs in advance is to cal-

culate your present total expenses—food, rent, car maintenance, clothes, taxes, entertainment—and assume that all your homestead costs will be about the same. While your mortgage payment or entertainment, clothing and food bills may be lower, other costs undoubtedly will be higher or entirely new—vet bills, extra fuel, tire chains, and seed. It is unlikely that your total cost of living—labor value plus cash—will drop drastically, even though you make a serious effort to cut expenses.

Another method is to make a list of the known, on-going homestead expenses: mortgage payment, food, animal feed, utilities bills, loan payments, auto maintenance, taxes, insurance payments, seasonal repairs and purchase needs. To this total add a certain percentage for the unexpected, as you did in figuring capital needs—perhaps 20–25 percent.

Many months or even years of homesteading may go by before you can get an accurate idea of your average day-to-day expenses. A series of crises or needed capital improvements will obscure the cost pattern of your routine enterprises.

Whether you have begun homesteading or not, the best way to keep your figures straight is to establish a convenient accounting system that will allow you to see just what your actual expenses are—where the money goes. Such a homestead accounting system (described later in this chapter) is especially useful if started *before* moving onto a homestead. Then you'll have a detailed picture of where and how your living costs change, up and down, when you begin homesteading.

## CASH SOURCES

We have already mentioned the need for savings, or some other kind of financing, for beginning costs. Perhaps you have a rich uncle who dotes on you, or you have access to family land. If so, you are in a fortunate minority. Most people have to scrimp and save to meet initial expenses, and they have·to find a satisfactory means to continue earning a living once they are settled in the country.

### SOURCES OF CAPITAL

Besides using savings, raising the needed capital usually depends on selling already existing assets—a house, car, stocks or a business. This is a sound and obvious move, except that few potential homesteaders are financially secure members of the affluent society. Most, therefore, expect to put most of their savings toward a down payment on a house on a few acres and to find new means of income to meet the subsequent expenses.

## WORK: THE HOMESTEADER'S DILEMMA

As a beginning homesteader you face this real dilemma: You need to work both for cash and for yourself. How can you do both the homestead work and a job outside, that seems so necessary? How can you find the right balance between buying food and raising it, or between hiring a repairman and doing the repairs yourself?

If you are working fairly happily now, perhaps you would do best to continue working for a regular salary until you feel more confident to start your homesteading. Just as likely you are fed up with your regular job and can't wait to begin the practical, full-time work of building your own place. Whichever it is, you will probably find that some sort of compromise—a transition period—is the most practical route.

One compromise may be to work in a small city or town while building your homestead nearby in leisure time. (Ed Robinson did exactly that while he was working on the *"Have-More" Plan,* except that he commuted into New York every day!) Another compromise may be to leave your staff job and work in your old field as a freelancer, or to build up a freelance practice in the city in preparation for a move to the country. Whatever the arrangement, you'll probably regard it as a necessary evil, to be endured only until your homestead is on a solid footing. This early transition period is one of the most difficult parts of establishing a successful homestead.

Once you actually move onto your land, the problem is somewhat different. If you keep a job you may find yourself frequently wondering where you will find the time for important home chores and improvements. If you do not, you may worry about finding cash for tools, lumber, taxes and mortgage payments. With an eye to the future, you probably will conclude that *some* cash enterprise must be established that will provide for the reduced but persistent demands for cash. If you wish to stay in your local area and to maintain your homestead work time, essentially you have two choices: (1) develop a home product or service, or (2) learn a skill that you can sell in your new area.

# ON-HOMESTEAD WORK

## HOMESTEAD PRODUCT

*Animals.* Some homesteaders bring in needed extra cash by selling products from their animals. If you keep chickens, you should have several dozen eggs to sell every week, as well as occasional chicks or hens. If you have even two cows, you may be able to bring in a little cash selling milk to friends or neighbors (though generally you will not be permitted to advertise the sale of raw milk or deliver it). Cows also have a tendency to produce calves, which you also may sell. Other animal products might include wool from your sheep, goat milk, ducks, honey, puppies (if you have dogs) or rabbits. The list is long, and you may enjoy raising a certain breed specialty as a source of income. A list of booklets with further information is given in the chapter appendix. (Also see Chapter Four.)

*Crafts and Cottage Industries.* Some homesteaders have craft skills that are particularly well-adapted to country living. Potters, for instance, can live practically anywhere; they can market their work through city stores and make supply trips to their outlets every few weeks. Other craft works that often fit well with rural life are weaving, jewelry-making, metalworking, glass-blowing and wood-carving.

A certain disadvantage for craftsmen who live in the country is the distance to their customers and distributors, since local sales usually aren't enough. But this is not insurmountable, and many craftsmen are enjoying the lower living costs and the peace of rural life. They sometimes find it difficult to divide their time between a craft and homestead chores; in fact many work practically full-time at their craft and maintain only a marginal sort of homestead. Others, of course, run a wild and woolly farmstead and do other work only as needed to supply enough cash income.

A variation on this kind of individual craft operation is a communal homestead "cottage industry." Most of the many communal farmsteads in this country for survival have developed some sort of community enterprise. *Twin Oaks Community* in Virginia, for instance, manufactures polypropylene hammocks, which it ships directly to customers. *East Street*

*Gallery* in Iowa manufactures specialized photographic print-washing equipment. In both cases, the members of the community work part-time at the commune industry, which continues regardless of turnovers in membership. This sounds unusually businesslike, and we'll discuss the management of a homestead business shortly. (See also Chapter Seven for a discussion of communal homesteads.)

*Other cash products.* There are many other cash-producing homestead products, not strictly crafts, that we haven't mentioned. One example, maple syrup and maple sugar, often is a good source of income for New England and Middle Western homesteaders. Another might be wood—for fuel, lumber or pulp—if you own a large woodlot. Other possibilities should occur to you, too—products that are available in your area and which are saleable. Some of these homestead products might be:

> apple products
> baked goods
> pickles and jellies
> sauerkraut
> honey
> vegetables
> seedlings
> nursery plants
> furniture
> weaving

### HOMESTEAD SERVICES

Another means of earning cash is to provide a service for which customers will come to your homestead. You might run a small sawmill part-time, for instance, or a blacksmithing or welding service. Perhaps you're good at car mechanics or seamstress work. In any of these cases people may come to you, providing you with a ready-made source of cash (or other products, if you enjoy using the barter system). You may develop some close friends as well.

Naturally the few ideas given above don't exhaust the list. (See chapter index.) If you're an editor, a writer or an illustrator, you may be able to sell your services on a freelance basis, making occasional trips to the city to visit publishers. Then again, there may be local publishers or print-

ers, or local newspapers that would appreciate your services from time to time. In any case, you would be able to work at your home much of the time, and to plan this work around the daily chores and small crises that arise.

## OUTSIDE WORK

### LOCAL PART-TIME JOBS

Unless you are a professional person such as a lawyer or psychiatrist, you probably will regard outside work as somewhat undesirable—perhaps justly so. It usually requires regular hours and takes you away from pressing work at home. So I am speaking of *part-time* work, and assuming that a full-time job is incompatible with homesteading (except perhaps in the case of a large family or group, where one member works full-time to provide the family's cash needs).

The problem with rural, part-time jobs is that usually they are rigorous and pay very little, as any woman who has worked as waitress, secretary or sales clerk in a small town can testify. Such jobs often are scarce, too, in spite of the high turnover, because there still is a large number of people in country areas who have little education or training that will enable them to do better. And there are many, perhaps like yourself, who specifically do not want full-time work and will take whatever part-time job is available.

## OTHER ARRANGEMENTS

But if you have specific skills it often is possible to arrange part-time work on a better basis. For instance the local printer may well need an experienced typesetter or proofreader at peak times. The local schools will need occasional substitute teachers. Or an engineering firm might welcome drafting or surveying help when they have an unusually large job. Shop owners may need periodic bookkeeping help. The possibilities are limited only by your imagination, energy, ability and, naturally, the area in which you live.

After you have lived in a community for several months or years you will meet the craftsmen, businessmen and professionals who work in your fields of interest. You'll make friends, and if you work dependably you'll find your skills or services requested.

Finding your niche does take time, though. And at the beginning it also takes energy and a certain sense of how to approach people. It's a good idea as a newcomer to be deferential—not to push yourself forward too soon. People need to get to know *who* you are, not just what you say you can do. As a new resident you may be regarded with a certain suspicion despite your best intentions. In short, no matter what your city experience, go slow in approaching a local business with your irresistible offer to help. Do offer, but remember that you have to prove your good character and helpfulness like any beginner. (See Chapter Eight for the differences in relations among country people.)

## HOMESTEAD-RELATED SERVICES

One good source of outside income may be work related to your homestead chores. If you have high carpentry skills, for example, you may find

part-time work on other people's houses or work when needed for a local contractor. Neighbors may need help cutting timber, surveying, putting in water systems or doing roofing. Sometimes orchard owners need apples picked or trees pruned—seasonal work that occurs in your particular area. Other possibilities are hauling (if you have a good truck), cutting wood, helping with maple sugaring, haying, driving a school bus or snowplow. There really is no limit to such local possibilities, though often they produce more barter opportunities than cash.

As with more conventional part-time work, some ingenuity is a great help in discovering or inventing the sort of service that is most suitable

for you and is needed locally, too. Be sure you know your own skills, personality, the demands of your homestead, and the community's wants. Something to remember here, too, is that if you decide to offer your services you risk less than when you gear up to produce a product.

As you live in your new community for a while, you begin to see what products or services are likely to be in demand. You'll become more familiar with the varied ways of earning a living in your locale; you'll make friends; you may even have sound ideas for income that no one ever thought of in these parts.

Following, to help spur your imagination, is a list of services that often are in demand in small rural communities:

Carpentry
Stone building and concrete work
House construction
Rototilling
Tree cutting and other forestry work
Fireplace maintenance and chimney cleaning
Haying
Fire warden work, forest fire fighting
Butchering
Basement excavation and general earth moving
Tree nursery work, growing seedlings and greenhouse plants
Teaching, either privately or as a substitute. Private tutoring
Typing and editing services
Sign painting
Surveying
Bookkeeping
Appliance repair

## TRAINING

If you are young enough not to have mastered or begun any particular career, you have this advantage: you can choose a craft, skill or trade that is particularly well-suited to your homesteading area. For example, few people today know how to build with stone in New England, even though fieldstone is probably the most common building material to be found. (In some fields, it seems more evident than the soil!) So you might consider acquiring skill at stone-masonry, particularly at building walls and fireplaces. This is the sort of skill that likely would be in steady demand, but would not tie you down to set hours or require a special education and professional obligations, like being a doctor or dentist. (Doctors and lawyers and dentists also are much in demand, everywhere, but they don't have much time for homesteading.) In this way, you would have enough work for your cash needs and have a very useful homestead skill besides.

Stonemasonry is just an example. Many, many skills are required for successful homesteading, and some of them are quite suitable as a source of additional cash income. Surveying, which Thoreau learned as an appropriate outdoor skill, is another. Carpentry, well-drilling, auto mechanics and tree cutting are all possibilities, depending on your own tastes and local needs. Less strenuous skills, such as bookkeeping, typing, and even publishing a community newsletter, also may be profitable.

The important thing when deciding on a product or service as a source of cash is to preserve a balance between your cash labor and your personal homestead labor. (There's more to this, which we'll discuss a little later.) You want to earn enough cash to meet your needs, but at the same time you must have enough time for essential—and some leisure-time—activities on the homestead.

Finally, remember that rural areas often lack many of the services available in a city. As an experienced accountant, barber or pianist, for instance, you may be able to move into an area where there is little competition, and earn a reasonable supplementary income by following your old occupation part-time. You'll be able to work shorter hours and enjoy a comparable standard of living in the country, where your living costs are lower. While you learn essential homestead and country skills, you can be marketing your unique city skills for a living. For more ideas about homestead livelihoods, read Milton Wend's classic, *How to Live in the Country Without Farming* and William Osgood's *How to Make a Living in the Country.*

## HOMESTEADING—A SMALL BUSINESS

When you buy your land and develop your sources of cash income, don't forget that you really are going into business for yourself. In fact, if you run a homestead and a freelance typing service, you really have two businesses! And being in business means keeping good records and accurate accounts, budgeting, keeping close track of costs and income, and generally learning to be a prudent manager.

Good records are important, partly as a basis for filing your income tax, and partly so that you will know exactly how you are doing on your various enterprises. Most people have good income records but don't do so well on the expense side. Full records are especially valuable as you experiment with different home systems, such as livestock feeding programs, maintaining your cars and trucks, building or restoring your home and erecting new barns. If you have fire insurance, an accurate and detailed inventory is essential. Likewise, if you need a loan from a local bank, a set of well-kept records will indicate care and businesslike attention to your affairs. Most important, when the time comes to judge the success or failure of your income-producing trials, having accurate information will make the assessment possible.

In his *How to Live in the Country Without Farming* Milton Wend describes a simple yet effective system for homestead accounts:

> A small change box kept in the house will take care of all cash transactions that take place at home. Keep two 3 × 5 cards in this box: cash paid and cash received. The Cash Paid card will contain the Date, To Whom, Purpose and Amount of each withdrawal. Make each entry promptly. Carry over the total to the heads of the cards as they are renewed. The difference between the sums of the two current cards should show the amount in the box at any time it is desired to check their accuracy.

## PRODUCTION RECORDS

Keeping accurate production records is just as important as your cash transaction accounts. For instance, clipboards with pencils on strings could be located in convenient places such as the chicken house, the milk room, the harvest room, the grain storage corner and so on. On each you would record produce harvested, pounds of milk produced and grain purchased or consumed. Each month these amounts could be posted to the various record books you keep.

The accounts you keep depends on what you're doing and how detailed you wish to be. Here are a few suggestions:

| *Expenses* | *Income* |
|---|---|
| farm overhead | outside income |
|   taxes | vegetable sales |
|   insurance | orchard sales |
|   payments | milk |
|   repairs | homestead services |
| outbuildings | eggs/chicks |
| roads and grounds | animal sales |
| fences |   rabbits |
| vegetable garden |   calves |
| orchard |   goslings |
| chickens |   piglets |
| bees | woodlot sales |
| pigs | honey |
| business travel | |
| household expenses | |
|   food purchases | |
|   staples and supplies | |
|   fuel | |
|   telephone | |
|   medical bills | |
|   life insurance | |
|   savings | |
|   clothing | |
| truck | |
| automobile | |

These accounts can be kept easily on large cards or single-entry pages, preferably loose-leaf. By taking a few minutes each week posting cash transactions and production records to these pages, you will have an accurate record of how well (or badly) each enterprise is doing. You may be surprised at how much it costs to make a trip into town, and then find ways to save trips.

One beauty of living on a homestead is your relative separation from cash. You don't need much around your homestead, but can keep a limited amount in a cash box, withdrawing what you need when you make trips to town. You're much less apt to fritter away cash unknowingly, as you might in the city.

## BUSINESS RECORDS

Keeping records for your cash enterprises is even more important than keeping your homestead accounts. As a self-employed person, your income tax form is more apt to be audited by the IRS, and you will need good records to substantiate your deductions. Very possibly, however, your business records will be simpler than your homestead accounts. Remember also, you may have to collect and account for sales taxes you collect on the products you sell.

If you run an illustration service, for example, you need only record your cash income and your expenses, which may be quite low. You would simply record your costs for drawing paper, ink, pens, lettering sheets, postage and similar office or art supplies, as well as the rent or mortgage portion for your home offices. If you order by mail, you have the returned check as a further evidence of your expense.

The same is true of slightly more complicated businesses, such as producing honey. You simply record cash expenses for equipment, veils, hives, any paid labor, honey tins and so on. The major problem is having the discipline to set down your expenses *as they occur,* and to save receipts, cancelled checks and other relevant data. Needless to say some rudimentary knowledge of bookkeeping is helpful in homesteading, but a fancy accounting system certainly is not necessary. It's far better to use a simple method that you can easily keep up to date than an elaborate one that continually falls behind and eventually fails. Just be sure to keep consistent records and to keep homestead and business affairs strictly separate.

USING THE BARTER SYSTEM

When recording income some arrangement should be made for the bartering of goods: such as exchanging your eggs for your neighbor's milk. A dollar value should be assigned to the exchange, based perhaps on labor value or current store prices. It is a good idea, here, to assign a value to your own time spent, so that you will have an idea of the real cost to you of the various products you produce, especially if you offer them for sale. While you are bypassing a cash economy in some ways, it is useful to see how you can convert your work into cash terms when necessary. Remember, however, that for the IRS your labor is *not* a deductible expense.

HOMESTEAD AND BUSINESS MANAGEMENT

Efficient management of your homestead and cash enterprises involves more than keeping good records of course. A well-managed homestead will require not only an efficient physical layout, proper tools, adequate storage and livestock housing, but also a sense of when to do certain jobs (and the steady discipline to carry them out). All of this boils down to careful and sensible planning.

*Physical layout.* As I mentioned in the discussion of housing, it is important to establish logical relationships among house, barn, garden, sheds, road and pasture. Consider the function of each room or building, the traffic patterns and the location of tools or supplies used there. This sort of planning alone will save many hours and many steps in a single year, especially in the kitchen, in a barn or crowded production area.

*Tools.* Another feature of the efficient homestead is having and using the right tools for each job. The initial expense of buying proper tools may be high, but it will be more than justified as your work is done quickly and easily in the years that follow. In Chapter Three is a discussion of basic tools, their care and storage.

*Livestock barns.* Keeping your animals healthy and happy is part of maintaining a smooth-running homestead. To do so you must have the right shelter and fencing for them, in addition to good feed and convenient water.

The kind of records for livestock production we have mentioned will allow you to calculate the profitability of your animals, to know exactly what you are spending on them, and whether they're worth it to you.

*Garden and fruit trees.* A good garden and fruit tree layout, consistent care and regular records kept on costs and produce, will tell you where to expand or cut back.

In all of these areas the important part of management is simply to establish logical ways of doing things and record what you have done—both what you put in and what results you have achieved. Rather than jump from one struggling enterprise to another, you are better off to concentrate your efforts on limited areas—for instance, to spend the first year on your house and garden only, leaving the animals or bees or a cash crop for following years. As some projects become successful and take less time, you will be free to add more activities to your productive homestead.

## PLANNING

What we are describing, of course, is a simple kind of planning—making conscious decisions about projects and then establishing a way to tell how they are doing. You always can give up what you have been trying and begin something new, or rearrange parts of your homestead for greater comfort and efficiency. One of the exciting parts of homesteading is that there really is no one way to go about it. Whatever you do is fine, if it pleases you and it works.

Since 1940 an immense amount of study has been given to work efficiency, including farming. The increased efficiency of the huge "agribusinesses" is one reason why corporate farms have steadily replaced family farms as food producers. And many experts say that, despite the poorer quality of the food, the huge farms are more efficient.

However, there is no need for your homestead to have quite the same efficiency standards as a business farm. You probably are homesteading because you prefer it, not because you expect to make a large cash return from it. You need to worry about planning and efficiency, despite all we have said, only to the extent that it makes your work easier and more satisfying, and perhaps gives you more time for other things. The kind of efficiency we mean is keeping the tools near where they will be used. Perhaps *common sense* is a better term for this sort of planning and care that you would want to do anyway.

## TAXES

Taxes already have been mentioned as one of the regular cash expenses of homesteading and being a property owner. However, you probably will feel that your tax bill is anything but routine, and in a sense you are right. Many farmers and rural families have been forced to sell their land because of their inability—not to make a livelihood—but to pay the property taxes! As the demand for country property increases, so do the tax assessments. You may have to make a yearly tax payment of $1,000 to $2,000 to your town or county—payments that you must prepare for most of the year.

Besides property assessments you also may face possible school, county or other special town taxes, state income taxes, and, of course, the federal income tax.

*Federal and state income taxes.* The IRS is more likely to audit the tax return of a home business or a self-employed person, as we have said. So it is doubly wise to keep good accounts and to be thoroughly acquainted with the legitimate deductions for your homestead business. These are some deductible items *if* your homestead is in business to sell produce or animals at a profit:

> auto mileage for business
> vehicle repairs
> wages for hired hands
> professional business services (lawyer, vet, plumber, forester, etc.)
> farm books and magazines
> membership expenses in farm groups
> all ordinary farm expenses (taxes, heating, insurance, telephone,
>    electricity, feed, fencing, lumber, etc.)
> costs of short-lived tools, equipment rentals and work clothes
> damage to property caused by natural disasters
> depreciation on buildings, vehicles, stock and capital assets
> personal medical and dental bills
> interest on business and personal debts

This considerable list is only partial. Your local IRS office or agricultural agent can give you further detailed information. Remember, though, that these deductions are only applicable to a business farm—*not* to a purely recreational or personal homestead—and you can qualify only by making a legitimate effort to sell your produce at a profit.

Similar deductions, of course, may be taken for other home businesses and their related business expenses. Craftsmen may deduct material costs, travel expenses to fairs, and advertising costs, for instance. Deductible expenses probably are more extensive than you think.

Remember, too, that home produce and home-made items are not taxed in your use of them, giving you an additional advantage when you make rather than buy the things you need and the food you eat.

## PURCHASING

There are many shortcuts you will want to take as a homesteader to reduce your purchasing costs to a minimum. The best two are to *make your own* (food, furniture, house, etc.) and to *barter* with friends or neighbors for products you need. Neither of these involves much if any cash. But there are other ways to cut cash needs, too.

*Auctions.* Local auctions sometimes yield real bargains, especially if you can resist the urge to buy a "bargain" you don't need. Those held in the spring or fall are more likely to have low prices than summer auctions, which often are aimed at summer residents and visitors.

*Mail orders.* Country dwellers have always found it convenient to order what they need from the large mail order houses like Sears Roebuck. Not only are prices relatively low, but the goods usually are designed for sturdy use. What's more, even today's high parcel post costs don't equal that of a trip to town. See chapter appendix for catalogs.

*Cash purchases.* Even when buying major items avoid store installment plans. Either pay cash or borrow the money through a local bank, which has lower rates of interest. If the bank won't lend you the money, think twice. Is it a good debt for you to incur if the bank won't go along? Charged purchases—if carrying charges are avoided—may be useful in establishing your credit rating, against the day you might really need it.

*Local stores.* Country stores sometimes have higher prices, but not always, and some things cost the same everywhere. The local store is likely to give more personal service, such as delivery, and it may prove a friend in time of need.

*Co-ops.* Farmers' cooperatives have been very successful in marketing and distributing the produce of members. Most co-ops are regional but some are local, and you will find out about them as you settle in. They usually have other advantages, too, such as available group fire and medical insurance. Often they also run stores and sell quality country items at low cost. *Food co-ops* also are popular in some areas. Through them member families join in making bulk food orders directly to wholesalers. They are especially useful for buying grains, fertilizer and similar staples in bulk.

*Second-hand goods.* A final suggestion (and you can probably think of others) is to buy most of your needs second hand from friends, at rummage sales or second-hand shops. Used cars, pianos, clothes, tools, furniture and appliances, if examined carefully for condition, will perform perfectly good service and save a great part of the store price.

## SUMMARY

Despite the complexity of income taxes and elaborate farm business records, homestead economics really are fairly simple. As you exchange city for a country life, you stop being just a consumer and begin to produce for many of your own needs. You learn to organize your garden and your other homestead enterprises in the most satisfactory way, and to take advantage of tax deductions. You devise accounting and production records not only to substantiate your deductions but to see how your homestead is doing. You continuously use auctions, rummage sales and bulk buying to keep cash expenditures as low as possible. You enjoy the homesteader's advantage of living well on a low budget, largely through your own ingenuity.

## APPENDIX

### SUGGESTED READING—BOOKS

Ball, Al
    Woodcarving for Profit. New York, Exposition Press, 1969. $3.50 paperback.

Chetwynd, Hilary
> Simple Weaving. New York, Watson-Guptill, 1969. 104 pp. $2.50 hardback.

Community Publications Cooperative
> How to Make Money Living in the Country. CPC, Box 426, Louise, VA 23093. Pamphlet

Creekmore, Betsey B.
> Making Gifts from Oddments and Outdoor Materials. New York, Hearthside Press, 1970. 224 pp. $7.95 hardback.

Drake, Kenneth
> Simple Pottery. New York, Watson-Guptill, 1966. 96 pp. $2.50 hardback.

Goodman, Paul
> People or Personnel. New York, Vintage Books. $1.95 paperback.

Handbook for Rangers & Woodsmen, Canadian Whole Earth Bookmobile, Box 6, 341 Bloor Street, West, Toronto, Canada

Harris, Kenneth
> How to Make a Living as a Painter. New York, Watson-Guptill, 1954. 142 pp. $5.95 hardback.

Hemard, Larry
> Leathercraft. Garden City, NY, Doubleday, 1972. 143 pp. $3.95 paperback.

Hobson, Phyllis
> Making Homemade Cheeses & Butter. Charlotte, VT, Garden Way, 1973. 36 pp. $2.50 paperback.
>
> Making Homemade Soaps & Candles. Charlotte, VT, Garden Way, 1974. 40 pp. $2.50 paperback.

Hopkins, John A. & Heady, Earl O.
> Farm Records and Accounting. Ames, Iowa State University Press, 1962. 377 pp. $8.50 hardback.

How to Buy Surplus Personal Property, U.S. GPO, Washington, DC 20402

Hunt, W. Ben
> Indian Silversmithing. New York, Bruce Publishing, 1960. 160 pp. $4.95 paperback.

Jobs in Alaska, Box 1565, Anchorage, Alaska 99501. $2.00.

Kirsch, Dietrich & Kirsch-Korn, Jutta
> Make Your Own Rugs. New York, Watson-Guptill, 1969. 56 pp. $3.50 hardback.

LaBlanc, Jerry
> 300 Ways to Moonlight. New York, Paperback Library 75¢

Martin, J. D.

The Home Income Guide. Vocational Educational Enterprises   $4.95.

Martyn, Sean

How to Start and Run a Successful Mail Order Business. New York, David McKay, 1969. 211 pp. $5.95 hardback.

Milmoe, James

Farm Roadside·Marketing in the U.S. Newark, DE, Food Business Institute, University of Delaware, 1965. 118 pp. $2.50 paperback.

Monroe, Ruth

Kitchen Candlecrafting. New York, A. S. Barnes, 1969. 172 pp. $6.95 hardback.

Mortenson, W. P.

Modern Marketing of Farm Products. Danville, IL, The Interstate, 1973. 364 pp. $8.50 hardback.

Nichols, N. P.

Profitable Herb Growing. Nichols Garden Nursery, 1190 North Pacific Highway, Albany, OR 97321. $1.00

Osgood, William E.

How to Make a Living in the Country. Charlotte, VT, 1974. 120 pp. $3.50 paperback.

Pearson, Haydn

Fifteen Ways to Make Money in the Country. Grosset & Dunlap, 1949.

Pfahl, Peter B.

The Retail Florist Business. Danville, IL, The Interstate, 1968. 435 pp. $10.00 hardback.

Shields, Earl B.

Raising Earthworms for Profit. Elgin, IL, Shields Publications, 1973, 127 pp. $2.00 paperback.

Smith, Clodus; Partain, Lloyd; Champlin, James

Rural Recreation for Profit. Danville, IL, The Interstate, 1968. 319 pp. $9.25 hardback.

Villiard, Paul

Raising Small Animals for Fun and Profit. New York, Winchester Press, 1973. 160 pp. $6.95 hardback.

Wend, Milton

How to Live in the Country Without Farming. New York, Doubleday, 1944.

Wigginton, Eliot (Ed.)

The Foxfire Book. Garden City, NJ, Doubleday, 1972. 384 pp. $3.95 paperback.

Foxfire II. Garden City, NJ, Doubleday, 1973. 410 pp. $4.50 paperback.

Wilson, Charles Morrow
    Let's Try Barter. Old Greenwich, CT, Devin-Adair, 1960. 184 pp. $4.95
        hardback.
Young, Jean
    Woodstock Craftsman's Manual. New York, Praeger, 1972. 253 pp. $4.95
        paperback.


## PERIODICALS

Second Income News (Monthly), Box 2506, Santa Rosa, CA 95405  $12 yr.
Workforce. Vocations for Social Change, Box 13, Canyon, CA 94516  $5
    donation


## EQUIPMENT CATALOGS

First New England Catalog, New York, Random House, 1973  $4.95
Gardeners' Marketplace, Box 2302, Norwalk, CT 06851
Gohn Brothers, Middlebury, IN 46540 (work clothes)
Last Whole Earth Catalog, New York, Random House, 1971.  $5.00
Montgomery Ward Company. (regional centers)
Mother's General Store, Box 506, Flat Rock, NC 28731
NASCO Farm & Ranch Catalog, Ft. Atkinson, WI 53538
Sears Roebuck & Co. (regional centers)

CHAPTER SEVEN
# THE HOMESTEAD COMMUNITY

The homesteaders of a hundred years ago were pioneers. They often lived on isolated backwoods farms for months at a time, seeing very few other farmers and rarely a traveler. Visits were few, since neighbors had to travel over poor roads. For long months winter snows made real self-sufficiency an absolute essential. Homesteaders simply had to be able to live alone on their land without close neighbors, social life, or anything approximating the modern entertainment of frequent community events, magazines, newspapers, radio and television.

When accidents occurred on frontier homesteads, home remedies had to do. In times of sickness or fire help often was unavailable or long in coming. Animals and people often died from relatively trivial causes. A broken leg could mean the loss of weeks or months of work—a situation that sometimes brought disaster. Families were kept together at close quarters for long periods, with accompanying quarrels, depression or bitterness. There simply wasn't a chance for much contact with the outside world.

In a way this isolation had some benefits. It tended to give early homesteaders a sense of their own strengths. It built self-reliance and confidence in their abilities to provide for themselves.

Admirable as complete pioneer self-sufficiency may be, few people today (though definitely some) wish to cut themselves off completely from friends, outside entertainment and community. In spite of home-steaders' desires to get away from the plagues of urban life, most still want a balance between the backwoods and suburbia. Unlike our predecessors, we do have a choice.

Among the many improvements in homesteading that have occurred since 1862, the change in communications is the most important. Radio and television have pervaded even the remotest rural areas, bringing news, weather reports and entertainment from the outside world. Sometimes we are even more aware of what is going on in the world than we would like to be.

But newspapers, radio and television mainly are links between home-steaders and the general urban community. None of these really con-tributes much to the life of rural families with a city upbringing—except perhaps to stiffen the new homesteaders' resolves to avoid city values. Other important means of communication, such as the telephone, have fostered the growth of true local unity and awareness among homestead-ers, and have changed homesteading from a very lonely life to one that can be warmer and less precarious.

The next three sections discuss the different ways in which homestead-ers relate to their immediate locality, to expanded homestead groups and to other homesteaders who may share the same problems and values.

## LOCAL COMMUNITY

In some ways, the local community is the most important cause of (or cure for) homestead isolation, for it is the focal point in any sense of community belonging.

If an entire area, such as a small farming town, shares homestead val-ues and attitudes, a sense of mutual support will bring people together. Milk can be bartered for hay, carpentry skills for seedlings or lumber and so on. In a small community especially, there usually is strong concern about a family in need. Somehow things turn out all right: the lost barns get rebuilt, the hay gets cut, the pigs get slaughtered. People tend to share and to look out for one another, even if they do it very subtly and deny it in public.

Even within a larger and less homogeneous community a smaller group of homesteading friends can give each other plenty of mutual support. In a semi-rural area homesteads tend to be small and neighbors not too far away. Neighborly sharing and getting together can become an important part of everyone's life. The capability for shared support and friendship replaces the austere need to be entirely self-sufficient.

Occasionally, of course, a person will settle in an area that regards homesteaders as vaguely unpatriotic. It may be a long time before he wins the respect and friendship of local people. At the same time, most rural areas have regional values and area identifications that run deeper than the matter of long hair or short. Being hard workers and good neighbors almost always will dissolve this sort of initial suspicion. In fact, you are likely to find that your neighbors become lifelong friends, particularly if they share your goals for homestead life. Most people in the country, after all, even though they may be cautious or cold at first, are receptive to new residents who share their choice of country living.

## CITY VS. COUNTRY RELATIONSHIPS: GOSSIP

If you haven't lived in a rural area before, you will discover some distinct differences in the way country people get along. For one thing, anonymity just doesn't exist. People in sparsely or moderately-populated areas not only want to know their neighbors, they also enjoy gossiping about them. There are very few secrets in a small town. Even in a scattered rural area, people not only will know more about you than you know yourself (you'll hear it last), but they'll be able to tell you all about everybody else and his parents and grandparents.

You'll also find that you must live in an area for many years before you will be considered true residents. No matter how long you have thought of yourself as an established homesteader or family, someday you will overhear yourself referred to as "that new family" or those "out-of-staters." It is frustrating, but there is nothing you can do except to demonstrate over and over your cheerful determination to stay and prosper. And after all, one of the pleasures of being a country old-timer is being able to look down on all the "newcomers" who obviously don't know much about what they're doing.

With your new neighbors paying such close (yet invisible) attention, you have to be careful not to make accidental enemies. In the country you are likely to have to live with the same people for many years, and it pays to get to know them before revealing too many eccentricities of your own. Country people tend to have very well-developed sensitivities and long memories. Show yourself to be steady, hard-working, and friendly; but do not try to create an intimacy that doesn't yet exist. In short, go slow in forging new ties. Give the neighbors time to look you over and decide how they feel.

## GROUP HOMESTEADS

One way to change the homestead community radically is to be part of an expanded or communal homestead. In the last six years, especially, many communes have come into existence which essentially are homesteads—in their attitudes toward self-sufficiency and their desires to live on the land. Expanded homesteads also include very small groups, of

course—perhaps simply one or two additional non-family members living on a basic or nuclear family homestead.

Whether you have four members or forty, there are many advantages to communal homesteading. The more members, the more hands there are to do the work—a built-in labor force. A communal homestead also has its own built-in social life: some people can make cider, some can talk politics (and drink the cider), while some can grow herbs or weave. While it has greater needs, a communal homestead also has more workers to bring in a cash income. The group is less dependent on the earning power and health of an individual. Some homesteads really have capitalized on this by offering their services as construction crews, haying teams, or by becoming an expanded cottage industry (see Chapter Five).

Other advantages may not be so obvious, such as on-the-spot babysitters, brainstorming sessions and mutual psychological support when the going is rough. More people will start more projects, contribute eggs, chickens, weaving, pottery, bookkeeping, typing, trips to town, cooking, plumbing or whatever their skills happen to be.

Expanded homesteads have their disadvantages, too. Many of the communes started in rural areas have disintegrated because of personal quarrels or lack of agreement on homestead goals. Having several members on a homestead often makes any single member reluctant to make decisions or take responsibility for general homestead work. The result is a predictable decline into disorganization, a lack of continuous maintenance work, untended gardens and the like. Naturally no one wants to pay for or do the work while others take a free ride.

An inevitable problem in the communal homestead is the setting of goals, the proper division of work, income and personal belongings. The most successful communes historically, such as the Oneida Community, the Roycrofters and present-day Twin Oaks, usually have had two extra features: (1) a shared philosophy or religion, and (2) a strong leader who could settle internal disagreements. While the first two communities now are thought of as failures, they did last for many years (Oneida dissolved only because of rebellion in the second generation). Communities whose members share only a desire for community are prone to failure.

While the Twin Oaks community does not have a charismatic leader like John Noyes (Oneida), it does have a precise organizational framework, provided by psychologist B. F. Skinner in *Walden Two*. Despite its

many differences from the book plan, Twin Oaks does manage to sub-merge inter-personal conflict into an overall system of homestead work and income distribution. It tries to eliminate any reasons for the members to be envious of one another. In some ways Twin Oaks' 50 members are not a homestead at all, but they do make an effort to be self-sufficient by con-tinuously reducing the amount of outside work performed by community members. Like any good homestead, Twin Oaks is businesslike in its con-duct of community economics, with the result that the members do in-come work only a few hours a day yet with good efficiency.

In establishing a group homestead, then, consider your shared goals and principles. If they are few, you should take other steps to reduce in-ternal friction and to make all members feel equally important to the homestead enterprise.

## GUIDELINES FOR GROUP HOMESTEADS

### MAKE SPECIFIC ARRANGEMENTS ON IMPORTANT MATTERS

The most important problem in any group arrangement is establishing an equitable system of responsibility. Even if you are only joining with others to buy land, it is vitally important that you decide in advance how the land payment is to be made and in detail how the land is to be shared. Such an agreement will prevent many later misunderstandings and quarrels.

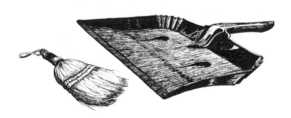

In a group homestead each member must feel that he has a fair share in deciding what projects will be undertaken and how they will be carried out. Also each must feel that the financial responsibility and rewards are equally (or fairly) distributed. Unfortunately, in spite of the appeal or just "doin' what you feel," such careful agreements are necessary. While they are painful to make, getting the operational decisions out of the way at the start will allow things to flow more happily later on.

## DEVELOP A SOUND ECONOMIC BASE

A second need for communal homesteads is the development of a particular homestead product or service. Twin Oaks' members share various aspects of hammock-making. Other groups produce more specialized products or work together on publications such as the Liberation News Service, or in group legal services. The production of a special homestead product or service not only may provide a dependable cash income, but will free group members from working off the homestead.

## BUILD NECESSARY BUILDINGS AND DWELLINGS

A third proposal for groups living on a commonly-held parcel of land is the building of separate dwellings. If members can afford to do so, having separate houses will tend to diminish the points of group conflict. Each person or couple will have his own sphere or mini-homestead, yet sharing tools, garden or workshops—perhaps even eating facilities. If cost is the major reason for joining together, the pooling of capital for a land purchase and the establishment of small separate homesteads probably is the most satisfactory and efficient arrangement.

If a group must live in a single house, follow the first proposal of establishing house responsibilities on a regular basis. Many communal homes become impossibly run down simply because the members do not have a distinct idea of who should be doing the cleaning, cooking and maintenance. The cooking gets done haphazardly. As a result the cleaning doesn't get done at all. This problem, as well as the hazard of personal power plays, can be avoided by getting group agreement on *what* should be done and *how* it should be done, though this decision-making sometimes degenerates into an endless gripe session.

## ENCOURAGE GROUP COMMITMENT

Most important in keeping together a communal house or homestead is shared commitment by the group. Some groups just seem to stay together without any political struggles. Other have constant internal wars and feuds going on among the members. But if the members have financial and emotional stakes in the group, this sort of thing can be kept to a minimum.

## DECIDE ON FIRM VISITING AND ADMISSION POLICIES

Another important point is to reach group agreement on group size and the admission of new members. Many communes have fallen apart because they felt morally unable to limit their membership or to turn away unwanted crashers. Group relations are difficult enough without everyone constantly having to deal with new members whose status is uncertain. And establishing a financially-workable homestead is so difficult in itself that unnecessary problems, such as the haphazard arrival of strangers, should be avoided. The best system has a firm group policy about crashers and new members (visiting fees, advance arrangements) that everyone follows.

## PLAN WHAT YOU WANT TO ACCOMPLISH. MAKE LEGAL ARRANGEMENTS

One more point worth making is that successful, long-term enterprises of any sort usually have a firm idea of what they are doing right at the start. They usually have made clear legal arrangements for financial and business matters.

Now this doesn't have to be the case. Some groups have managed all right running on personal good feelings. But vague legal definitions *usually* are an important reason for communal failure. When it comes to the crunch, people will walk away if it is easy for them to do so. If not, they tend to stay and work it out.

This all sounds heavily organizational and practical—quite the reverse of what many people have in mind in taking up a life of personal independence and cheap, earthy living. Unfortunately homesteading *is* a very practical sort of life in which you frequently must deal with gritty matters like legal arrangements, as well as septic tanks, building codes and goat fencing. Perhaps every communal homestead should have its own lawyer.

## PROVIDE A WAY TO EXCLUDE PEOPLE

Not only do people sometimes want to leave, but occasionally they may have to be asked to. If this happens, be sure to get the reason out in the open and give the whole community a chance to agree on whatever action is taken. Trying to ease someone out quietly only encourages paranoia among his friends, and makes everyone uncertain about what offenses are grounds for exclusion. A weekly general meeting keeps group friction above ground, and gives people a chance to air their gripes. Naturally the best time to solve a problem is when it first appears, not after it has festered for weeks.

## KNOW YOURSELF

From the very start, be sure that you really want to live with other people. Joining a commune because you can't afford to start your own homestead may be a mistake, if you are counting on keeping to yourself. Communal living requires group openness and commitment. If you really prefer being very independent, find another way to do it.

And if you want to *start* a commune, take a look at your motives. Are you really looking for other people whom you can boss around on *your* homestead? This sometimes happens, especially if one person owns a farm or piece of land and offers to share it with others. Almost always it is unhealthy for any one person to hold an unequal share of responsibility or financial power, because the imbalance prevents everyone from relating squarely.

A communal homestead, then, can be a good solution to the high initial costs and demanding physical work of individual homesteading. At the same time group living involves many additional problems. The many commune-oriented publications that offer further suggestions and information about actual groups are discussed in the next section. Others can be found in the chapter appendix.

## HOMESTEADERS—WHAT SORT OF PEOPLE ARE THEY?

Communes represent only a small fraction of the established homesteads, for those who prefer to live with others on a communal basis probably are in the small minority. Most homesteaders, as mentioned in Chapter One, prefer individual independence, though we have seen some of the advantages of group homesteads—more hands, home social life, financial diversity and mutual support.

Considering the rate of communal failure, the more independent spirits probably do better than their group counterparts in making their homesteads a success. At the same time the successful in either style seem to share certain attitudes and characteristics. Let's look at what they are.

①  *Successful homesteaders usually are people who would have succeeded (or did) equally well in the city.* Some worked for years in cities before moving to a more rural life. They learned how to be patient, how to save money for their needs and how to endure temporary setbacks.

②  *Successful homesteaders usually are people with strong interests or background in very practical work*—farming, carpentry, surveying, construction, mechanics and so on. This rule has exceptions of course: Scott Nearing was an economics professor before he moved to his homestead in 1932. But he had grown up in rural Pennsylvania, which demonstrates that a farm background is very valuable, as is a practical turn of mind.

Those *least* likely to succeed on the land probably are city intellectuals and political radicals who are consciously trying to prove the validity of another lifestyle. Homesteaders with a heavily theoretical approach tend to become disillusioned by the constant nitty-gritty work involved. In the end, most homesteaders live as they do because they enjoy it—*not* be-

cause they hold a strong political or theoretical viewpoint. Those who look for acclaim for their radical experiment usually quit in disappointment.

3. *Successful homesteaders have chosen their way of life and are committed to what they are doing.* This means, as we have pointed out, that they have *had* a choice of other successful ways to live. Seeing the alternatives, they have picked homesteading. They recognize that their choice may involve much more work and less income, but that it has other rewards which they prefer.

This background of success and chosen lifestyle means that homesteaders usually are strong people who know the demands of rural self-sufficiency. Often they are older than many would-be homesteaders; at any rate, they have had other experiences to teach them their own capabilities and values.

## SUCCESSFUL GROUP HOMESTEADERS

Obviously many group homesteaders share these characteristics with independent individuals. Forming and maintaining a group homestead takes equal determination. Besides overcoming natural obstacles, communal homesteaders must overcome internal disagreements. To enjoy communal security a group homesteader must be able to carry his share of responsibility for communal projects and finances. In many ways this imposes more difficulties than nuclear family homesteading, considering the countless group decisions that have to be made before various projects are done. The successful communal homesteader is a person who works well with other people and knows what he wants from the situation.

Independent homesteaders probably tend to be more antisocial than communards. They prefer to work things out alone and tend to have less trust of other people. Independence and personal freedom mean a lot to them. As a group, they tend to be older (30–50) than communal homesteaders (18–30). This grouping is very rough, but reflects the communal nature of today's back-to-the-land movement, as opposed to the more individualistic values of traditional country people. It probably is safe to conclude that most communes contain a high percentage of city refugees while people originally raised in the country tend to value the family homestead and its independence.

There is, in fact, considerable tension in some areas between traditional country people and the newer communal groups. The communes around Taos, New Mexico, are a special example of how "hip" culture can outrage and offend traditionally deprived rural poor. In general, communes are greeted with suspicion and hostility, but these feelings tend to dissolve slowly as the local people come to know the members personally. Most communes now make a special point of becoming involved in local volunteer work and social events—all good ways to win over neighbors.

### THE OLDER HOMESTEADERS

People who left the cities when the *"Have-More" Plan* came out now are in their middle sixties. They have been aware for years of the issues that environmentalist groups now are raising—the importance of growing their own food, recycling wastes and conserving resources. They are likely to own a small homestead and take pride in their independence from modern city life and their security in owning their own land at retirement age—even though they have no intention of "retiring."

### MIDDLE-AGED FARMER/HOMESTEADERS

While so many Americans rushed toward the cities after the second world war, some decided that farm life was what they wanted, even though they found themselves competing with increasingly · powerful agribusinesses. Many of today's middle-aged homesteaders intended to make family farming a success but found instead that they just about made ends meet. Most went into other income areas in the country.

Despite this lack of real farming success, they have tended to hold onto their land, maintaining the sort of home gardening and businesslike approach that we would regard as prosperous homesteading. These middle-aged farmers/homesteaders probably have the most to teach younger homesteaders in today's back-to-the-land movement.

### COUNTERCULTURE HOMESTEADERS

As a part of the complicated "counterculture" rejection of establishment values, thousands of college-age people have taken to homesteading as an alternative to higher-education's "good job" progression that was expected of them traditionally. Many, if not most, of these younger homesteaders have become involved in communal ventures simply because a commune is more economical and more supportive of group values. But many of the communes that were started in the late Sixties have long since failed—usually from a lack of commitment and discipline among the members.

People at age 18 or 20 who are choosing homesteading rather than schooling may be making a wise choice, but they face serious problems— particularly lack of savings and lack of experience and skills (depending on their backgrounds). Usually a communal situation or apprenticeship is the best way in which a young prospective homesteader (living and working on an established homestead) can learn the necessary skills while getting a taste of homestead life. As an age group these younger homesteaders are least likely to succeed, simply because of their lack of experience and capital. They tend to be unstable and uncertain of their goals. Homesteading often is a temporary escape from family pressures to get a college degree or to follow some more conventional family lifestyle.

As elsewhere, perseverance can overcome these problems, but it might be better not even to speak in terms of success or failure for young homesteaders. Their success is more apt to mean discovering what they want—and the answer may not be homesteading at all.


In the last few years a definite homesteading society has grown up, connected by common goals, problems and values. More and more people have forsaken city life and full-time jobs for a more integrated and simpler life on a small piece of land. With the willingness to try new places to live and unaccustomed lifestyles has come a corresponding willingness to join with others in communal living, both in cities and in rural areas.

While many homesteaders live in isolation, there are more threads of communication among homesteaders than ever before which allow them to share their information and experiences, and to learn from each other.

Homesteading remains a difficult life that demands not only capital and practicality, but personal determination and deep commitment. It also requires a personality that enjoys the challenges of rural self-sufficiency—that is at home with the everyday problems of country life and does not expect an ideal of rural bliss.

Not all homesteaders succeed. Some fail from too little savings, others from poor planning, still others from lack of application. Young homesteaders especially are unlikely to win through the immensely difficult tasks of learning country skills and establishing a place of their own. Those who do succeed usually are people who have had earlier successes, who know themselves, and who have chosen carefully the life they want. They are people who feel at home in relatively remote rural areas and who get along easily with their neighbors and fellow townspeople.

For all its requirement of independence and self-reliance, homesteading can be a life of very warm friendships and deep community ties. The opportunities for community exist on all levels, and more and more homesteaders find that they have much to share, and friends with whom to share it.

We live in a time when the tools for homesteading are all available—in fact when rising costs and other problems make homesteading an increasingly attractive alternative to American urban life. It is no wonder, then, that country dwellers are staying there, too, and looking inward more and more, toward their own regions as sources of livelihood and satisfaction.

# APPENDIX

## BOOKS AND SOURCES

Houriet, Robert
>    Getting Back Together. New York, Coward-McCann, 1971. 408 pp.
>        $1.25 paperback (Avon).

CPC, Box 426, Louisa, VA 23093
>    How to Start a Commune (pamphlet)

Leaves from Twin Oaks, CPC, Box 426, Louisa, VA 23093   $2.95.

Mungo, Ray
>    Total Loss Farm. New York, Dutton, 1970. $1.25 paperback (Bantam).

New Community Projects (news)
      32 Rutland Street, Boston, MA
Skinner, B. F.
      Walden Two. New York, Macmillan, 1960. $2.25 paperback.
Spiritual Community Guide
      Box 1080, San Rafael, CA 94902. $2.95 paperback.


## PERIODICALS

The tremendous growth during the last few years of the back-to-the-land movement has been matched by the appearance of many magazines and journals aimed at country and communal people. Some are more suitable for beginners, others to long-time homesteaders; most all are entertaining and informative. The best thing about the publications that follow is that they provide a forum for people with similar ideas and hopes and means to be in touch with one another. Here is a description of some of the basic homesteaders publications and how to get them.


*Alternative News,* Alternatives Foundation, Route 1, Box 191, Oroville, CA 95956.

*The Better World News* is a short newsprint magazine that comes out whenever the editors (T. Sawyer and B. Thatcher) feel the need. It is a good source of information about books and other magazines related to healthful country living, though largely it reviews, reprints and condenses other sources. It's particularly good for material on nutrition and inexpensive ways to live. Paradise Publishers, Box 88, West Point, CA 95255. Cost: $.25 an issue, $3 for 12 issues.

*Clear Creek* is a serious environmental monthly that comments on various events and environmental happenings from a literary and radical political position. It can be entertaining and politically informative, but contains no real practical help on environmental homestead problems. A typical feature article might describe an environmental conference or cover a regional issue, such as logging in the Northwest. Clear Creek Associates, Inc., 1 South Park, San Francisco, CA 94107. Cost: about $8 a year (11 issues).

*Communities* magazine is published bi-monthly through the efforts of several communal groups, including Twin Oaks and the Alternatives Foundation. Its viewpoint is mostly the communal lifestyle—how to make a commune work, how actual communes are doing. It gives addresses of specific communes, rather than "how-to" articles. *Communities* emphasizes specific aspects of communal living—the role of women, public relations, selecting new members. While it is not completely relevant to the individual homesteader, *Communities* is an exciting account of the relations among new communal homesteads. Community Publications Cooperative (CPC), Box 426, Louisa, VA 23093. Cost: $1 per issue, $6 per year.

*Country Living Magazine,* 4302 Indianola Avenue, Columbus, OH 43214.

*Countryside: Small Stock Journal* is a short near-monthly (ten issues a year) for those raising livestock, such as rabbits, goats and chickens. It has information about new breeding techniques, feed, pens, markets and meat cuts, as well as a breeders' directory. It carries features also on general aspects of homestead life and plenty of classified ads. *Countryside* was established in 1917 and can be ordered from 318 Waterloo Road, Marshall, WI 53559. Cost: $5 for one year, $9 for two.

*The Green Revolution* is another small journal, published ten times a year. Unlike *Mother Earth News,* it is more concerned with building the real counter-culture community, featuring articles on conferences and schools and community organizing. It also carries thoughtful articles, personal accounts and book reviews. It has very few personal ads. Published by Heathcote Center, School of Living, Route 1, Box 129, Freeland, MD 21053. Cost: 40¢ an issue, $4 a year.

*Hawthorne Homestead Report* is one of the more modest new newsletters. Essentially it is an account of the doings of a couple on their "Hawthorne Homestead"—more of a printed letter to friends than anything else. All the same, it contains useful, first-hand information about homesteading for the beginner or prospective homesteaders. Write to HHR, RD #1, Nunda, NY 14517.

*Homesteader's and Landcrafter's Newsletter* is a particularly entertaining and informative little magazine, first published in 1969. It consists almost entirely of letters from readers—very folksy and full of interesting tips and tales. Ideologically it is rather right-wing, backwoods stuff, but still useful and fun to read. Wildcrafters Publications, RR 3, Box 118, Rockville, IN 47872. Cost: 35¢ a copy, $2 per year or 6 issues.

*The Mother Earth News* is probably the best-known of today's homestead publications—a bi-monthly journal of "how-to" articles, recipes, letters and personal advertisements. The drawbacks to *Mother* are its extremely short (and consequently frustrating) articles, and its calculated appeal to "gentle, back-to-the-land folk." Despite these criticisms, *Mother* has much interesting material, especially for people who haven't yet gotten a homestead established. The Mother Earth News, Box 60, Hendersonville, NC 28739. Cost: $1.35 an issue, $6 per year.

*Natural Living* is a monthly with broader interest, featuring articles on nutrition, childbirth, gardening and childcare, as well as book reviews and recipes. It has no classified ads. Natural Living Magazine, 1560 Broadway, New York, NY 10036. Cost: $9 for 12 issues.

*North Country Anvil* is a small radical journal similar in size (24 pages) to *The Green Revolution*. It has articles about alternative enterprises, literature, cooperatives and homestead-related skills. Emphasis is on radical economics and organizing as conventional communities. It doesn't come out regularly. For information, write to *North Country Anvil,* Box 252, Millville, MN 59957. Cost: $3.25 per year, $1 for back issues.

*Organic Gardening and Farming* is one of the basic gardener's magazines and probably is of interest to most homesteaders. It has excellent articles about organic gardening techniques, specific tips and stories and homestead-related subjects, as well as book reviews and ads. Organic Gardening and Farming, Organic Park, Emmaus, PA 18049. Cost: $6.85 a year (monthly).

*Your Land* is a quarterly entirely about buying land—what brokers' terms mean, what to do, what to avoid, how to get a mortgage and so on. It also has a few related articles—perhaps plans for a sauna or tips on renovating old houses. It also describes specific areas of the country for land availability, prices, job opportunities and the local government. Dugent Publishing Corporation, 236 East 46th Street, New York, NY 10017. Cost: $1 an issue, $4 a year.


## OTHER COUNTRY-RELATED PERIODICALS

### GARDENING, LANDSCAPING

American Fruit Grower
American Vegetable Grower
Better Homes & Gardens
Family Food Garden
Farm Journal
Flower and Garden
Natural Gardening
Progressive Farmer
Southern Living
Sunset

CARPENTRY, WORKSHOP & CRAFTS

Craft Horizons
The Craftsman
Creative Crafts Magazine
Family Handyman
McCall's Needlework & Craft Magazine
Mechanix Illustrated
Popular Mechanics
Popular Science

LIVESTOCK & FARM EQUIPMENT

Countryside & Small Stock Journal
Electricity on the Farm
Farm Journal
The National Future Farmer
National Livestock Producer
Today's Farmer

CHAPTER EIGHT

# HOMESTEADERS SPEAK
# FOR THEMSELVES

WEST SWANZEY, N.H.

"In defining what we're doing here I find it hard to apply any words beyond those of 'making do.' People leave the city and go back to the land for many reasons—maybe as many reasons as there are people doing it. The one big motive seems to be a desire for freedom to work out their own lives. But all people don't have the same resources, personal or economic.

"Some people can afford to buy a working farm or an abandoned farm and get directly to the work of implementing their self-sufficiency, if such is their goal. At the lower end of this order, however, you find people only able to afford the rudest of land. Their task is very different. They are closer to the edge of civilization. They are more akin to the American pioneer in that they are literally faced with cutting out a home in the woods. This is more or less what happened here.

"Whether you can really call this a 'homestead' or not is a moot point. People in town call it 'the hippie camp', which may have applied

219

three years ago but no longer does. Hippies don't stay around long. Nor is it a commune, though there is more than one family.

"What it is is simply a bunch of people sharing a piece of land. There is some sharing of labor, but each family takes care of most of its own necessities by itself—wood supply, money, machines, tools, etc.

"There are three separate gardens which in the past have been planted and maintained communally and the produce shared. It looks like this coming year, because of more people living here, each garden will be handled by a few people—one family—but the produce will be shared. A crisis such as a car getting stuck or a lot of snow needing to be shovelled, brings out a community spirit and sharing of the labor. We hold community meetings as the need arises. Lately it has been agreed to hold a monthly meeting to improve inter-family communication.

"We presently are faced with a problem that has nothing directly to do with homesteading, but which other homesteaders I'm sure will encounter—namely the hassle over local building codes.

"Our problem is largely of our own making. When people first moved onto this property three years ago, nobody even thought to check with the town about building codes. They just thought that because they were way off in the woods miles from town they could build anything they pleased. And it was so. The town simply chose to ignore what was going on here as long as we didn't bother them.

"This year the imminent arrival of two babies during the snow season brought two of the families into conflict with the town over the plowing of the mile of old town road leading to our property. The town felt that if we expected such services of them they could in turn expect us to adhere to their codes—the main bone of contention being our "illegal" outhouses. The solution to this problem will not be an easy one.

"It might be wise advice to future homesteaders not only to look into local building ordinances before building, but perhaps even before they buy. Building codes are, on the surface, designed to protect people against unscrupulous building practices. But more often than not they are used to exert political control over the humble freedoms of people like you and me."

## DOBBINS, CALIFORNIA

"Sam and I were happy city dwellers who would spend weekends, whenever possible, in the country. One weekend we came back to Berkeley, looked at each other and asked: 'Why are we coming back?' Two months later we had quit our jobs, sold our home and car and found a beautiful place in the country. Our friends were shocked, as we had never discussed the desire to move—because we didn't truly have it!

"We lived here alone pretty much for one year and had a glorious time doing the country things. We did miss people, and so came up with the idea of starting a community—not a commune—of people who would be close enough together physically and mentally to share tools, labor, ideas, child care, shopping trips, good times.

"There would be no rules, by-laws or pre-conditions of any sort except that each family would own its own plot and be financially responsible for his/her own family.

"Sam and I originally had purchased 80 acres, and when we came up with this idea we purchased an additional 40 to re-sell in 5-acre pieces. Many people came out, and at this point eleven families have bought land (our eight pieces plus three nearby), and two families are renting. Only six families live here full time, but more are planning to move up this spring. We have enjoyed seeing our idea become a reality. As we share our survival trip with one another, we have grown closer, formed some deep friendships, and are thoroughly pleased with all aspects of the community.

"We have had limited experience with communes and saw the problems created by people who were out-and-out leeches on the rest of the group. An interesting side effect is that we are growing more communal. We want to do a communal garden this summer, and we are looking for some method for communal income production. Sam has recently completed a woodshop and we are looking for some product that we can all turn out—perhaps working six months during the winter and then take six months off from it—or some sort of arrangement where no one is working the eight-hour-fifty-week grind of the past.

"The 80 acres we still own is available for the use of anyone in the community. Some people who have five acres may want to do a large garden or keep animals. They can use our land. This spring we are building a lake which will be our community swimming hole. Oh, we do have one rule here: No shooting. All our friends are more than happy with this rule.

"What can be done without? One family—formerly from the Los Angeles suburbs, complete with their own business and all consumer conveniences—is living happily (father, mother and two wiggly boys) in a 16-foot dome. They are doing without just about everything. They originally planned the dome as a temporary shelter and go back to L.A. for the winter and come up in the spring to build their home. They never went back, had their furniture stored in the barns of various people here, and have postponed the building of their house indefinitely, finding they truly enjoy the new way.

"One family designed and built a 900-square-foot house—quite nice— for about $1,500. They have gas stove and piped water. For the house used lumber was found and other lumber purchased from a small mill. They got around the building rules by applying for a permit to build a storage shed, and when it was completed they simply moved in. Requirements for building a house are much more complex and, naturally, expensive. I think it is important to check out the local building inspector and try for some kind of cooperation, or they can be nasty. There is always some way to meet their demands reasonably.

"Finding the *right* land is not as difficult as finding the right land *nearby* or large enough to accommodate the kind of people you want as neighbors. Many people really don't know what they want. They have some vague notion of country land with trees, and with chickens running around. So it's important to have some definite ideas like whether or not one wants a large garden, range land for animals, what weather conditions suit, the right soil and drainage.

"Another question people must ask themselves is: At what level do I wish to exist? Our friends in the 16-foot dome are happy at that level, but

I freely admit that I like the convenience of electricity and indoor plumbing. So it will take much more energy for me to be financially self-sufficient than they. I am willing to pay the price.

"Another question that should be raised is: Why am I leaving the city? People who leave for negative reasons—such as pressure from the establishment, bad relations with people, and who are angry, depressed or generally unhappy with their lives in the city—99.9% of the time are angry, depressed and generally unhappy in the country. The environment docsn't make a bit of difference. You carry your Self wherever you go. Those who have come here seeking to build something positive, wanting a more peaceful environment, wanting to be closer to the land, may have their low moments, but they can weather the bad times and generally are quite happy most of the time.

"Our house is a wood frame building, one story with three bedrooms, living room, large kitchen-dining area, screened dining room (where we eat all our meals from May through October). Our office was formerly the garage.

"The place was built about 16 years ago by an older couple who enjoyed fixing up homesteads. They also planted many beautiful trees and shrubs. But by the time we found the place several tenants had left it a mess.

"We were able to buy the place at a good price and have fixed it up quite a bit. There are several other buildings—a smaller house where our three older sons live. There's a barn, separate garage near the barn, a small storage shed between the houses and a larger one above the garden area. All the buildings were run down, but we have fixed them up and are using all of them. We have electricity, water from our own wells and telephone.

"When we moved here we intended to buy land and build our own place—and perhaps one day we will when our family is grown and gone. When we found this place, however, we realized we couldn't possibly buy the materials and supply the labor (considering our labor has some value) for the price of the buildings and the 80 acres that went with it. Although the house and buildings aren't ideal, we are quite happy and plan to stay here for a long time.

"Two sets of friends living here have built. In both cases they lived on the land in minimal shelter to get the feel of the place before building. One family planned a dozen or more houses in several locations before they finally decided what to build. They took into consideration the pattern of the sun, the shade, view, proximity to the rest of the land and neighbors, and ended up with a beautiful place which they built themselves with help from friends. It is 400 square feet downstairs with a 200-foot loft upstairs and separate bath house. It cost about $2,500 for materials.

"We all use wood stoves. We have an Ashley which has to be the finest wood stove available. It heats our entire house quite adequately with normal stoking twice a day. Our first year all we had was a fireplace, and we froze for five months.

"We have a septic tank and most people do, as it is required by the county. There is not enough population density for a sewer system. Two families here have out-houses and plan to compost their waste and use it on their gardens. This is against the County Health Codes, but they are doing it anyway.

"The land here is gently rolling foothills at about 1,700 foot elevation. There are a couple of cattle ranchers, many retired people, many commuters and a few homesteaders—and everyone we know has an organic garden and a desire to keep the land here beautiful and unpolluted.

"The area is moving in the direction of 'recreation land', because a large dam was built near here three years ago creating a 17-mile-long lake that attracts motor boating-fishing people, who like to have week-end places, and also retirement people. It would be difficult for anyone to make a living from agriculture here because land costs and taxes are so high. We don't foresee high density population here, however, because we are 150 miles from the San Francisco Bay area and there are recreation areas much nearer S.F. A recreation subdivision about a mile from here went bankrupt, and we all applauded.

"Our ideal is to have enough food for the whole year. Three years ago we planted 36 fruit trees, and each summer I learn more about gardening and our likes and needs and how to preserve food. I did mostly freezing the first two seasons but last year did a little canning, which I feel preserves certain fruits better (in terms of flavor and space), and we want to try drying this year. We are far from self-sufficient in our food production at this moment.

"My husband and I have real estate licenses, and our major work is to help people like ourselves find land and start homesteads. We help ourselves through bartering. I make clothes and Sam makes bee hives, for example, which we trade for goats' milk, furniture, etc. We buy at thrift stores when possible and buy new tools and equipment jointly with our friends, and share. Our friends work part-time as carpenters, handymen and at crafts. We will probably always have to do something on the outside to generate a little cash. Sam and I have found that although we don't have the material needs of most city people, we still need fences, tools, car parts and animal feed, and they all cost money. But as we are more established our needs for cash should continue to diminish.

"On buying land communally: From our limited experience we find that people really enjoy owning their own little plot, be it ever so humble. To me the ideal situation would be for a group to pool their money, buy a large piece and then split it up so each family has its own piece, with perhaps a large communal area that all can share. It saves a lot of money to buy a large piece of land. For example, there is now available for sale here a beautiful 485-acre ranch with creek, two houses, and a lake for $350 an acre. If it were subdivided by a wheeler-dealer it probably would sell for $1,500 to $2,000 an acre.

"If a group considers buying in a large piece and splitting it among themselves, there are important details to check, however, regarding local subdivision laws, survey requirements, road, utility, sewage and water requirements. The costs of all these can be exhorbitant in certain areas, especially California. Also don't forget building codes and zoning ordinances. Even we back-to-the-landers have Big Brother watching in many areas."

COLEBROOK, N.H.

"We signed papers in October of 1961 on 200 acres, an old house with attached ell and two old barns. We made the big final move up in August of 1962. Arthur got work as a foreman in a small plastic factory and I started farming and having children.

"The years were hard up here at first. We had hardly any money to do with, the winters were very long and cold and the house was old and cold. So for someone who didn't belong here in the first place I can see why Arthur's disposition got worse.

"We had a rough time with the property settlement because he wanted to sell the whole farm. In the end I kept the back 100 acres and let him have the big white place on the hill, with its high mortgage and taxes. When he went full time at the post office he had hired a contractor and crew to do all the work on the place that he could have been doing, and we had ended up with a new mortgage of $19,000! This was in 1970.

"So the kids and I now have four years more left on a lease on these buildings and the land. Then we must have it all together on our back land, to move onto it and create a new homestead. My advice to any would-be homesteaders about to make the move: be sure both husband and wife want to do this kind of thing and do it together. Otherwise it's just no good.

"I did manage to keep my farm animals in the property settlement, as I had always been the one to care for them. Right now I'm down to two milking cows and have two Jersey heifers. I raise veal calves in the summer but have found out the hard way not to start any this late in the year. There are about forty chickens in the hen houses and a dozen ducks under the old barn. I also have two rabbits, two geese, six guinea fowl, two dogs and five cats. Stuart has his pair of draft horses here too.

"I met Stuart a year-and-a-half ago when he and three other guys bought a nearby farm. Stuart has since left their partnership in Massachusetts to live up here, and he's been with us since last winter. He's having trouble making money up here and is working part-time at a ski area. He hopes to be able to do more in the carpentry line and also work in the woods more with his draft horses. This winter he's busy up back on my land getting the logs cut and yarded out for the cabin and barn that has to be built in the next four years. We're supposed to get all the logs cut by spring and the cement work and foundations in by this fall.

"We have a huge garden that gets bigger every year. There's an unlimited demand for certain vegetables, and I sell a lot. Homesteaders can easily make extra money selling surplus vegetables to local people. I board dogs and cats for folks, too, and that brings in close to $500 a year alone. You just run an ad in the local paper.

"Here's some specific advice. On finding land: Send for every real estate catalog you hear of. Pick an area and send for copies of the local newspapers. Write to any and all real estate advertisers in those papers. This should open up a lot of pieces of land to look at. We found our place listed in the big Strout nationwide catalog. Land prices were much different then. We got this place for $5,850, and now land is going for $100 to $150 per acre in large lots. Finding land is relatively simple. It's finding the money to pay for it that comes harder.

"Even back in the sticks money is a necessary evil. So many folks dreaming of becoming homesteaders feel that they'll be able to become self-sufficient right away. I've got news for them. It just doesn't work that way. Even all the things you need to help you become a little self-sufficient cost money. I've been eleven years and I'm still not able to live off the farm, although our cost of living is much less than any of my friends who aren't farming.

"If a person has enough cash in the beginning to buy and completely pay for all his land, buildings, farm equipment, animals, seed and anything else he's going to need to farm—and enough to supply his needs for the first ten years—he *might* be able to be self-sufficient right away.

"An outside job is almost a necessity. Today's costs just to stay alive takes care of most rural incomes even though you are efficient and economize at home. You learn to be a 'low income family' and to like it."

GARBERVILLE, CALIF.

"We've been here since last October, although we spent the summer before looking for land and some of the time here. I won't say we are or aren't homesteaders, as I really don't know what one is.

"We have 43.87 acres of steep hills and trees. There's very little open area, and what there is is small and far between. There is plenty of all-year water, which is important in this area where it rains all winter but not at all in the summer. The land was logged twice—once for tan oak and again in the '30s for Douglas fir. It was done selectively, so didn't hurt the land too much. There's plenty of wildlife, too.

"We located this land with the help of friends who told us about this area. Tom knew he wanted to be in the Pacific Northwest but didn't know exactly where. We came to look around and after a few weeks of heavy hiking and camping on various pieces we decided on this one.

"We paid $11,000 in cash. You can usually get a better deal with cash and also won't have the hassle of monthly payments. The population here has doubled in the past three years, and land prices have gone up five to ten times in cost in the same time span. I'd say that as long as there are people looking for land, prices will keep going up.

"Now we are living in a 16-by-20-foot cabin, actually a 'storage shed.' The building code for a dwelling was too heavy, and so we called our structure a storage shed to make life easier. Except for agricultural buildings you need a permit here. Most people ignore the code, but you can run into trouble there too.

"We built the structure ourselves with only hand tools. It took three weeks—not bad in the rain! The front wall is seven feet and the back fourteen, so we had plenty of room for a sleeping loft. The cost was $700. Lumber was at its most expensive then, and we could have done it for less by getting used wood from old buildings. But we didn't want to spend the time taking them down. Before we built the cabin we lived in a tipi— but that's another trip altogether.

"The only real problem with the house is its location in the trees, where there's very little sunlight. Eventually we'd like to build a dome on the ridge. We planned to use this building as a workshop. The only problem we didn't foresee was the building code department.

"I dislike the lack of open land on our piece. We also dislike the access road—mud in winter and dust in summer. But that will be taken care of this year when it is graveled. We hope to improve the soil for gardening, and our present project is to plant areas that are eroding.

"Neither of us has an outside job. When our garden starts yielding in a few months and our baby chicks start laying eggs and our pig grows some more, we'll be more self-sufficient than we are now. We plan to have goats soon, but all these things take time. I'm too busy getting these trips together to wonder about being self-sufficient.

"I don't know if we've gotten through the hardest part. We made the adjustment to country life pretty well. We've got a roof over our heads and friendly neighbors to help us when we need them. There's always more work to be done and always will be. Neither of us can foresee leaving, but anything can happen, and we know many people who have left in various stages of getting their homesteads together. A homesteader has to be willing to do a lot of hard work and put up with many inconveniences. One also needs to have a good imagination to come up with country solutions to everyday problems—in being able to look in that junk pile and see how that scrap of metal can be used to fix whatever needs fixing. You need to know many skills (cooking, building, sewing, plumbing, gardening, etc.) or be willing to learn. A mistake that is made by beginning homesteaders like ourselves is to underestimate the amount of work involved.

"If a couple has $5,000 saved, they should try to make sure they can make it on that sum. It depends on how much land they want and the many expenses. If purchasing land under terms, make sure there's a way to make money.

"There are very few jobs here—many people are on welfare, food stamps, etc. Tom and I had quite a bit of money saved, and he's mechanically skilled and can make some money while helping our neighbors. We also barter frequently or exchange labor.

"My favorite parts of homesteading are that I love living in a building I built with my own hands. I adore our animals (most of the time) and feel a real thrill when I see a bit of green pushing up out of the soil.

"Some things aren't as much fun. These include burying our water line, turning over hard-packed soil studded with rocks. On the whole, though, the good outweighs the bad 100 to 1. If things got really rough—meaning it were impossible to survive here—I suppose I would grudgingly go back to the city. But this life is my choice.

"I doubt if we'd do anything differently if we were to start again, since we had the advice of our neighbors to help us realize problems and avoid them."


LANCASTER, N.H.

"The log cabin I'm living in (18 by 30 feet) with a cathedral-type roof, cost approximately $4,500 for materials. The cost could have been reduced by using rough-cut lumber or (more appropriately and less expensively) real logs for floor joists and roof rafters, by using more efficient roll roofing, by using second hand windows and a minimum of wiring.

"So I think the cost could be brought down to $3,500 or $4,000, including septic system and water set-up. Of course there are variables which will affect the cost, such as the expenses of a well, septic system, distance from road of electricity, etc.

"My wife and I plan to build a real from-the-forest cabin this summer, using nothing but trees on location for everything possible. We hope our costs will not exceed $3,000, as we will have town water at hand, and experience, which is a greater teacher. The more we get into building the more we realize how we can cut costs and time.

"We're into a commercial type thing at present in an attempt to raise money to pay off our mortgage and move into (build) our "dream house" out in our meadow—a spot where we hope eventually to live off the land as much as possible—by living as simply and practically as can be done.

"In our speculating encounter right now we're building a home where we expect to put in perhaps $9,000 or $10,000 for materials, all inclusive. And we'd like to sell it for somewhere double this cost. We have a friend who has built a log cabin for $11,500 and has sold it for over $25,000. So you see costs are fairly relative to the type of cabin you want to build.

"Variables which affect costs are the kinds of windows, roofing, plumbing (copper or plastic), flooring (polished or not, carpeted, etc.), types of appliances, cabinets, heating. I'm sure you get the idea.

"As to time, I'd say six months would be a good estimate to be on the safe side—this is with one person doing all the work himself, including cutting the trees. Cost of trees for a 20-by-35-foot cabin would come to $300 to $500, depending on the extent of use of logs for floor and roof construction. To me this seems prohibitive, so I suggest either renting a tractor to haul logs yourself and (if at another location) having a logging truck haul logs to the site. Or better yet, as I did, buy an old twitch horse. I paid $300. Cut and haul logs yourself at the site and then use the horse on the homestead to plow, clear land, stumps and rocks.

"I find our horse well worth the price we paid, due to the great number of things I can do with him. Renting a twitch horse is another possibility. Usually the charge is low—under $10 a day, perhaps $5. I'm presently lending my horse out to work in exchange for his room and board.

"In our commercial venture I've chosen to stretch construction time out over a full year to finish this house, but only to be able to do a number of other things at the same time. I see no reason why you could not build, suitable for living, by three months, and then finish up as you are living in it.

"The building all can be done by one person. That is, one person and two block-and-tackle setups on tripods. Twenty-five to thirty-foot logs can be handled by one person. Naturally on some aspects of the job a friend would come in handy, like putting up a ridgepole. But these jobs can be saved for a time when friends are available. I think a husband and wife team is a good combo to do this job—setting up a homestead, working together from start to finish.

"Logs are easy to build with as far as structure is concerned. They are naturally heavy when moving, but once in place you know they're going to stay, and it's built to last! Leveling the logs is not difficult. Chinking can be homemade. We mix clay, straw and mosquitoes. It's all a natural endeavor and very satisfying. I think that anybody who has attempted his own cabin is happy he did. All that matters is that a person *wants* to do the job."

ORLAND, MAINE

"I've been in Maine for five years supporting myself by stonemasonry and sometimes writing for the *Maine Times*. I'm not homesteading because I don't have any land of my own. Wish I could afford some.

"In that time I've seen a lot of homesteaders come and go, and I'm afraid I've developed a less-than-healthy cynicism about most of them. All but a very few, I have noticed, are subsidized by money from their upper middle class parents, trust funds and such, and also by the poor and working class Maine folks whose taxes go to pay for surplus foods and food stamps. Often homesteaders spend all their time gardening and fixing up an old farm, putting the place into luxurious repair by local standards. This is called by them 'farming.'

"Meanwhile, their native neighbors down the road manage to garden, keep their houses in fine shape, get all their wood in for the winter, and spend eight hours a day working for the state, plowing and maintaining the roads. Even the be-overalled homesteader would be stranded without the straights who plow the roads.

"Most disappointing, however, is the homesteader who brings to Maine, in his attitudes and prejudices, all the places he hoped to leave behind.

"Since I've been here land has gone up 500%. No exaggeration. The more it goes up the faster it sells. I have come to feel things go in cycles. The homesteaders react as sensitive people do when they see the entire country being strangled by shopping centers. You and I do too. But their personal solution follows another cycle up here: 1. Old couple on fixed income taxed and high-costed off the family land into a trailer on three acres. 2. The other 97 acres go to a realtor for $7,000 and then to an out-of-state homesteader for $21,000. 3. The new owners, having sunk their entire stake into the farm, go on welfare—to the amazement and sometimes resentment of the local people. 4. The younger, native generation of Mainer, who might have inherited the family place, long since has moved to the city, where they try to make a living and escape to the suburbs.

"My wife, who has just read this, says it's too one-sided. But I guess you get the other side from more enthusiastic homesteaders.

"As you have probably imagined, I am as guilty as any, of some of the naïveté and shortsightedness that I've put down. In a way we're somewhat self-sufficient. Or try to be. We cut our wood, put a deer in the freezer every fall, raise a pig or two, garden. I'm sure we live a lot better than a lot of people in the cities and on a lot less."

LISBON, MAINE

"I don't strictly speaking classify myself as a homesteader, for we make no attempt to claim that we live off our acreage. We remain tied to the utility companies and supermarkets, and have been very conservative to our approach to 'getting back to the land.'

"My husband and I are both natives, but we are from the southern tip. We knew nothing of gardening or animal husbandry when we moved to our farm (large in house and small in acreage) two years ago with two young children.

"First we acquired a mare (lovely to handle but she couldn't be ridden). We knew nothing about horse care, and they require plenty! In the fall she was replaced by an excellent gelding. We were given one chicken, which now lays one egg a day. We bought a retired trotter who pulled a sleigh or wagon and on occasion large rocks or a dead tree. We planted a huge garden, we've pitched a lot of hay and shoveled and spread a lot of manure. We want more hens and a lamb in the spring.

"We've done nothing unusual except perhaps sticking with it. I've seen city hippies come—and go. I've read *Mother Earth News* and other similar publications, and one thing is missing. We are creating a myth and a very harmful one. It is: That it's easy to farm, that it's natural and that you'd know how if you could get in touch with your inner self.

"To that absurd notion I say you can no more be an instant farmer than you can be an instant computer programmer. It has to be learned one day at a time. Books can't save you from losing your livestock to an overnight disease. Only the farmer next door can tell you whether a frost will be killing.

"Gardening is back-breaking work, grooming a horse is time-consuming, and hauling water to the barn is a drag. You can only make it if you love it or are remarkably stubborn. To start out with animals you've never taken care of before is folly. Finding land is one thing. Paying for it is another.

"People didn't leave the farms originally because they couldn't stand eternal bliss. It's hard work and it is not for everybody. If only you could tell people that you have to fetch the egg before you can eat it, then maybe those who leave won't feel so defeated. Those who stay, on the other hand, will know that the negative feelings they experience are just part of it. It's a mixed blessing, like most things, but the feeling of virtue won't hold you over the first winter.

"These pearls of wisdom are from someone who's just beginning. Seek out people who are more than summer soldiers. Find a couple of people who tried and failed. Find out why. There is more to be learned from them, perhaps, than from the others. The more I learn, the more I realize how much I don't know."

DIXMONT, MAINE

"We are here because we were able to obtain the environment, the tools and many resources and implements for the kind of life we wanted, to live by cooperating and sharing with my parents. It was my project partly because it was my parents and their lives we were getting involved with— and because I had a stronger view of the physical home we could enjoy.

"Benjamin has not had a strong direction in terms of material aims. He does not have a clear feeling about the values and creativeness which he would like to express and live with.

"Having a full-time job is a means of obtaining money now at the time we need to spend it—on the house, farm equipment, etc. But the aim is for eventual establishment of essentials, expenditures to be minimized and income to come from our work on the land and in the workshop, and probably short-term jobs in the community (in carpentry and designing).

"There is certainly a lot of friction between my mother and me. I don't believe generations living together is at all ideal, but I do believe there is enough continuity and similarity in our life ideals and values that things could work out. Benjamin is a little less sure of this than I am.

"But we—Ben and I—are willing to give it a try. Having our own home will be a good step toward seeing if we can share the land and cooperate with each other as individuals.

"There is no way that you can foresee that constant proximity can cause friction, or to plan for it, life and people being what they are. There are weeks on end where you work together constantly, and the sharing of daily life is not stifling, but rather enriching. There are times when a partner needs to be alone. But these times need not be artificially created, for often partners are separated by the nature of the work. Sometimes I am cooking or sewing while Benjamin is out pruning fruit trees. Even last week when hauling manure and spreading it, there were times of aloneness for each, as I sat on the tractor while Ben pitched away."

### HARMONY, MAINE

"We have many friends who are homesteading, and every one of us has a different idea of what he wants out of it. Some of us are making a go of it and others aren't, but more are staying with it than leaving it.

"The important thing is to decide just what you *want* to do, and then do it. Make a master plan and then follow it. As you go your ideas may change—ours did—so then change. Who is to say there is a right or wrong way?

"We haven't found anyone yet who can make a go of it and not work out. Most of us try to work in the winters, as summers are pretty busy. There are taxes to pay, registrations and licenses, supplies you don't grow, and feed for animals runs expensive. You can live without animals, but we chose to live with them. We feel they pay us back and then some for our labor for them.

"Our master plan was to buy from fifty to a hundred acres with a woodlot and pasture and a house barely liveable, until we could build our own log house. We planned to get out our own logs from our own woods for the house. We also had to have wood to burn for fuel.

"We had to stay within a $7,000 limit for the property. We felt we couldn't handle a mortgage, so cash it had to be. We ended up settling for fifty acres. The house is small but the repairs were minor for temporary living, and hopefully they will last until the log house is ready to move into.

"We moved in the first of April and foolishly bought a cow, chickens, rabbits and a team of horses, and had no place to put them. So a barn was a must before snow fell.

"We hauled our timber out of the woods with the team and built a pole barn. Words can't tell of the hard work involved, but we sure are proud of our 40-by-40-foot pole barn. We had friends over for a good old-fashioned barn raising. We wouldn't have made it without them.

"Labor Day found us penniless. We had gone through $4,000 since April first. But we both got jobs and hope to take the summer off to start our log house.

"We are trying to grow as much of our own food as we can. The cow gives us milk, and in turn we churn our own butter and make cottage cheese, cream cheese and block cheese that varies in taste from cheddar to Swiss. Our cow also produces a beef critter for us, we raise rabbits to eat, our chickens give us fresh eggs and meat, we raise a pig, and we have five hives of bees for honey, raising buckwheat for them, which we also reap for ourselves.

"We make all our own bread and plan to raise our own winter wheat. We also want to build a methane digester to cook with and run a hot water heater in the summer, as well as to run our vehicles on.

"We have electricity and running water. I started with a pump but found we needed too much hot water. I find running water gives me more time to do other things that I wouldn't get done.

"Once our house is built and our pasture land has been re-seeded we feel we should be pretty independent and should live very nicely on $2,000 a year. We don't go on vacations or long trips and don't have luxuries. We have a plain, simple life that keeps us busy, happy and at peace with our world.

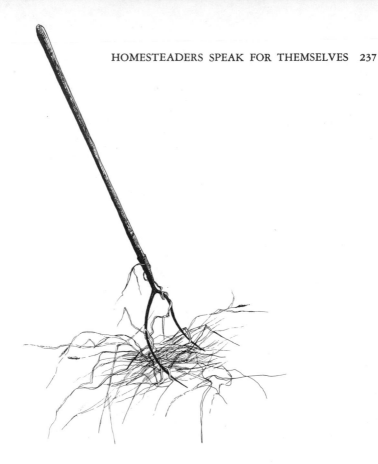

"We have two teen-aged daughters who weren't very happy when we moved here last year, but they love it now. It brought about a change in them that sure pleases us. They know what hard work is, what team work is, and what goes into the food we eat.

"I could go on and on, we are that enthused, but I think I have hit the highlights. It *is* hard work, but *most* rewarding."

ONTARIO, CANADA

*How long have you been homesteading?*
One year.

*What size is your place and sort of land is it?*
100 acres mixed bush, 2 acres cleared, much swamp, some good sugar maples and hardwoods. In short, cheap land.

*How did you locate your land? How much did you pay? Have prices gone up since?*

$3,500. Prices up a little in four years. Be sure to have your boundaries checked. We were shown a nice lot next to us but unknowingly we bought the swampy lot next to it.

*What kind of house do you have? Did you build it yourself? At what cost?*

Log house made from fir trees, peeled, fiberglass chinking in between each log for tightness. Good and warm. $250 for nails, flooring, roofing.

*Do you feel your house is well suited to the land? Any regrets? Problems you didn't foresee?*

Blends as well as can be for a house. We lived in a tipi while I built the house, and the tipi has many beautiful aspects, warmth not being one of them. It was difficult to find enough trees because most of the land within living distance of civilization has been recently logged. You see old pioneer homes still intact after 100 years with timbers hewn that are larger than most trees today. Gone is the virgin forest. But smaller logs are easier to handle.

*What do you dislike about your place or hope to improve?*

If a piece of land is not outrageously priced there is something wrong with it and you won't be long in finding the worst things. Our place has a lot of rain, which is not fatal in itself. But heat, water and Canadian bush equals mosquitoes.

*Do you have outside work? What kind? Can you foresee a time when you could be self-sufficient?*

Yeah. We do crafts, leather, weaving. I don't know what self-sufficient means. We all need each other. The buffalo is gone. I like to need other people as little as possible, and as time goes on we become better and better at surviving on our own. There is a lot to learn. This area with its short garden season prohibits non-cooperation with people, which means money. You can't grow enough for yourself unless you set up as a farmer, but farmers are all specialists, exploiting a specific cash crop. Also there are always things like car costs, machinery upkeep, as well as accidents and emergencies. Our goal is not to get away from the world but to learn as much as we can about as many things as we can.

*Do you feel you've "made it" through the hardest part of getting a home-stead going? What length of time do you think is crucial for those who are going to stick it out?*

Four full seasons. We pitched our tipi on a small patch of soaked moss in a field of snow in May. That spring and summer was as bad as any could be—rain, killing frost in June, mosquitoes in clouds, rain, dysentery, heat and more stinging, biting bugs than I ever believed possible. Building my house alone with a scarlet tanager and a divine meadow lark for company, plus our determination to do what we set out to do kept us going. I've told about the bad things. There were many beautiful times. Yes, I think we are over the worst, because now we know what we can do. Self confidence. It's just life. What else is there? The city?

*What characteristics do you think homesteaders should have?*

Various, divers skills, determination and most of all a sense of humor. A good working couple can do the work of five singles. You've got to *love* physical labor. No office clerks.

*What mistakes do you feel inexperienced homesteaders usually make?*

Like I said, about getting your land surveyed. But remember to believe that you can get through somehow. And you don't *make* mistakes. You *learn* whether you do it right or wrong. I don't think, though, that you can survive too long with mistakes. You learn quickly that mistakes are costly at best and at worst are fatal. At first it takes a while to get out of your previous life style and into the homestead, on-your-own trip, but once you hit your stride you're home free.

*What advice have you to give a young couple just looking for land with $5,000 saved?*

Have some way to get more dollars. Five grand'll get the land but you need to live, you'll need to put in money and work and time and blood before "Your Place" is your place and will help support you. Cut your expenses to a minimum, then cut them again. Since I started I quit drugs, alcohol, cigarettes, many things. We spend money only on food, tools, material for crafts. We buy bulk natural foods, vegetarian, no luxuries. So we don't need much money.

*Besides finding good land, what advice would you have for people just moving onto a new place?*

Test the drinking water. Measure the water level so you'll have an idea what it does next year. Buy an old Ford farm tractor (would you believe ours is a 1939 model and runs like a top?) if you want to do any work. Horses are nice, but unless you can hire them they take a lot of care, the time for which you won't have for a while. Survey your land in detail so you'll know what you have and where you have found it. On an open farm this is simple, but bushland is thick and takes a while to learn about.

*What part of homesteading have you liked most?*

The sense of measurable accomplishment. There are results from what I did last year. Now I live in a house that I built with my own hands.

*What have you hated most (or had the hardest time with)?*

Mosquitoes. Though I hear you can get used to 'em in time, I don't believe it yet!

*If things got rough, would you go back to the city for a job or city life?*

One does what one must. I prefer the wilderness to the city, but I hope by the time things get rough it won't bother me at all.

*If you were starting again, would you do things differently?*

No. I can't dig retrospective self-punishment. I just do the best I can every day, and it hasn't let me down yet.


"Like any undertaking its success is not immediately measurable. It takes years to see if one's actions are as they should have been. But we are very happy doing what we like to do outdoors in the woods. Our livelihood is marginal at best, and I don't know if we get ahead with each work-filled day gone by. But who gets ahead anyway? We're happier than most! We drink clean air.

"We have almost no cleared land, but we hope to get a pair of goats and some chickens this year. I would also like to get a work horse, if I find the time to build a barn. But remember animals tie you to a place.

"We're still eating now in March. Yes, we can save some. This year we will save more because we know what to plant. Ask local people what to plant. An old farmer befriended us too late to help in the garden, but the wealth of information in his head is simply staggering. Not all have this gift. Such a true gift is a rare thing.

"I realize that the field we are looking into is vast, the number of interesting ideas legion. Perhaps that is why this life is so full. People ask in the city: 'But what do you do out there?' All I know is that I'll never finish exploring the things that I want to look into. Life: the more you get into it the more there is."

# INDEX

Stonemasonry, 186
Stoves
  gas, 158
  kerosene, 158
  wood, 154-156


Taxes, 42, 192-193
Terrain, 57, 160
Tipis, 77
Tool shed, 89
Tools, 54-55, 89, 96, 136-137, 166, 190


Underground houses, 77-78
Utilities, 57


Veal calves, 125-126


Water, 38, 57, 67
  locating, 144
  power, 162
  purity, 39, 144-145
  quality, 39, 145
  rain, 146
  storage, 146
  systems, 139-144, 146
  wells, 141-144
Wild foods, 115, 118
Wind generators, 162
Wood
  cash crop, 180
  firewood, 83-84, 153-154
  precautions, 156, 165
  storage, 154
  stoves, 154-156
Wood frame houses, 72-73
Woodlot, 36, 40-41, 153

## ABOUT THE AUTHOR

Author David Robinson first became interested in homesteading techniques as a Boy Scout. Later, as a student and graduate of Middlebury College, he lived in a primitive cabin in Vermont, surveying and cutting trails on historic Mount Independence.

In the course of his research for this book, David visited with homesteaders in several eastern states and corresponded with others in almost every area of the country and Canada. Many of these letters are reprinted in this book, as well as specific answers to his questions about homestead life.

For several years, Dave has worked as a freelance writer, as well as a book designer. He has also been active in book publishing as an editor and currently serves as production manager with Garden Way Publishing in Charlotte, Vermont.

Dave has recently started raising rabbits and looks forward to having larger animals on his own homestead in Vermont in a few years.

## ABOUT THE ARTIST

Artist Paula Hartford Savastano, raised in Sherborn, Mass., at age 13 moved to Boothbay Harbor, Maine, where she graduated from high school in 1962. She attended Colby College and The Museum School in Boston until opting for marriage and going back to Maine.

Recently Paula returned with her husband and three children from three years of homesteading in Nova Scotia to their present home in East Boothbay, where she is working on two children's stories and an account of the family's Nova Scotia experience. She is as much involved with music as with art, and is an active member of two Canadian music associations.

# OTHER GARDEN WAY BOOKS
# YOU WILL ENJOY

*Raising Rabbits the Modern Way,* by Robert Bennett. 156 pp., quality paperback, $3.95. Everything for the home and semi-commercial produced.

*The Family Cow,* by Dirk van Loon. 270 pp., quality paperback, $5.95. A wealth of information is offered with clarity.

*Raising Poultry the Modern Way,* by Leonard Mercia. 240 pp., quality paperback, $4.95. Outstanding in this field.

*Raising a Calf for Beef,* by Phyllis Hobson. 128 pp., quality paperback, $4.95. Not only how to buy and raise your calf, but complete instructions for butchering and cutting beef for the home freezer.

*The Canning, Freezing, Curing & Smoking of Meat, Fish & Game,* by Wilbur F. Eastman Jr. 220 pp., quality paperback, $4.95; hardback, $8.95. Authoritative, easy-to-follow directions.

*Keeping the Harvest: Home Storage of Vegetables and Fruits,* by Nancy Thurber and Gretchen Mead. 208 pp., quality paperback, $5.95; spiral bound, $6.95; hardback, $8.95. The best of all the food storage books.

*Build Your Own Stone House,* by Karl and Sue Schwenke. 156 pp., quality paperback, $4.95; hardback, $8.95. All the information you need to do this.

*Down-to-Earth Vegetable Gardening Know-How,* featuring Dick Raymond. 160 pp., 8½" x 11", quality paperback, $5.95. A treasury of vegetable gardening information.

These books are available at your bookstore, or may be ordered directly from Garden Way Publishing, Dept. BHS, Charlotte, Vermont 05445. If order is less than $10, please add 60¢ postage and handling.